The G.I. Prince

Prince Franz Hohenlohe

The
G.I. Prince

A pleasant assortment
of narrative vignettes about
some of the special people
and unusual circumstances
encountered in the eventful life

of

Prince Franz
Hohenlohe

with a modest selection
of related photographs from
the collection of the author.

EVENT HORIZON PRESS

The G.I. Prince

Library of Congress Catalog Card Number 93-73009.
ISBN 1-880391-08-2.

First Printing, January 1995.

Typography and Design by Joseph Cowles.
Photographs courtesy of The Hohenlohe Collection.

Published by:
Event Horizon Press
Post Office Box 867
Desert Hot Springs, California 92240

♾ Printed and bound in the United States of America.

With thanks

to all of the people

who have made my life

so beautiful.

F. Hohenlohe

THE CHAPTERS

This is how it all began

My name is Franz Joseph Maximilian Rudolph Weriand Stephan Anton zu Hohenlohe Waldenburg Schillingsfürst—what people in America, where I have a home and spend half of every year, call "quite a mouthful." As far as Stephan and Anton are concerned (Steven and Anthony in English), it may be the other way round: Anthony Steven. I frankly can't remember. And yet it is I myself who chose these two names. At my baptism? No, hardly. At my confirmation.

I was confirmed at Oxford, when I had already reached the ripe old age of sixteen. A real scandal. And how is it, I can hear you ask yourself, that my parents, who after all were good Catholics, did not have me confirmed in the innocent flowering of a younger age? I think they simply forgot. And, if the truth must be told, I think they also could not have cared less to have an unconfirmed offspring bounce around in the world.

My Father Confessor at Oxford, however—the famous Monsignor Ronald Knox, much-read author of thrilling detective novels that sold like hot cakes—thought otherwise. He thought poorly of having one of his flock run around unconfirmed in the quads of Magdalen (my college). And quad, by the way, means quadrangle. Oxford slang. He had me confirmed.

On that solemn occasion I was allowed to add two

1

further Christian names to the ones I bore already. I was delighted, for five Christian names is not much in my family.

I opted for Steven because, though born in Vienna, I was Hungarian. And Saint Steven is the patron saint of that country. Yes, I know: a Hungarian Hohenlohe. That may seem strange. Perhaps, if not too lazy, I shall explain this phenomenon in a later chapter. I also found the name of Steven doubly appropriate because my uncle Constantin Hohenlohe was the one who, during the crowning ceremonies of the last Hungarian King, in Budapest in 1916, carried the Crown of Saint Steven on a velvet cushion during the procession. This Bishop Hohenlohe was my uncle, my father's brother. My cousins—his three children—live in the Argentine. And if it seems equally strange to you that a Catholic Bishop should have three children, or even two, or one, I shall explain that in a later chapter.

As for the name Anthony, I chose it because that Saint stands high in my esteem. Or perhaps it's the other way 'round and I rank high in his. However this may be, I am a constant loser of car keys, sunglasses and sundry other possessions, which Saint Anthony, most obligingly, returns to me 90 times out of 100, against a small donation. So I thought, perhaps rather perfidiously, that I would ingratiate myself with him by choosing his name.

On one occasion, however, Saint Anthony behaved quite shamefully toward me. To make matters worse this was in Padua, *his* city! And right plum in front of his basilica to boot, where I had parked my car while I disappeared inside to say a small prayer. The car I owned at the time was a Chrysler convertible, and since it was the middle of summer, the top was down. Beside me, on the seat, I had left a small square pill box. (I must here explain that I avoid pills like anything. But I do swallow vitamins in quasi-industrial quantities. So a pill-vitamin box to hold them is essential.) On the lid of this charming little box was a medallion of . . . you won't believe this: Saint Anthony.

When I came back out of the church the pill box was gone. No doubt the thief had thought that the box was of real gold, which it wasn't. Imagining the discomfiture of the thief when he discovered this was my only very un-Christian consolation. Saint Anthony never returned this box to me. Really very mean of him. I didn't speak to him for quite a while after that.

After all these preliminaries, you will certainly want to know my age. Such impertinence! My age is none of your business, because at my age one has reached the age where one is old enough not to have to divulge one's age. Besides, you can always consult the Almanach de Gotha.

For this book is not, not, not a biography. How could an unknown nonentity have the insolence to write his biography? Biographies are for record breakers such as Elizabeth Taylor, but not for me. What this book is all about is people of note I have come across in my eventful life.

And now please turn the page.

Dramatis Personæ

Mil: Abbreviation of Milla. Abbreviation of Ludmilla. An abominable Christian name which all of us in the family abhorred. I was the one who did the abbreviating. The mother of my mother: Mrs. Hans Richter, later Baroness Kálman Negyessy de Szepessy, a name she had difficulty remembering, which one can well understand. A very special human being.

Pop: My polo-playing father. Occasionally with an eyeglass in his eye. Rectitude was his middle name.

Steph: Happened to be my mother, among many more important things. Her name of Stéphanie Juliana had also been shortened, but not by me. By her chum Kathleen Vanderbilt.

Ernst: One of our two footmen, later butler. Or so it says on paper. But in reality a sage, a playmate, an adviser, a rare and precious pearl.

Steph, The Fabulous Princess.

*Pop—leaning on the Rolls-Royce
belonging to one of his ex-wives.*

Anna: Steph's personal lady's maid. Always clad in darkest black. Far more Catholic than the Pope. Far more royalist than any King. Alas— I must confess—also very anti-Semitic.

Peter, Mary, Podgy, Katja and Pepinella:

Five skye terriers whom Anna called globally "the boys."

Gaston: Our French chauffeur. He taught me how to drive, when I was seven, sitting on his lap. The first tree I ran into stands in Ouchy, Switzerland. Gaston was only allowed to drive our French cars, a Chenard & Walker and a Hispano-Suiza. The eleven Rolls-Royces which followed were driven by . . .

Mostyn: Who was English. Mostyn played golf with us, the family. Much better than we did. He had been chauffeur to World War I Prime Minister Lloyd George, and knew 10 Downing Street inside out.

The Trojan Horse

Right after World War I, my family, starved I suppose for fresh milk, trains which ran on time, and well heated hotels, spent much time in Switzerland. It was *the* country for recovering from war-time hardships—especially when you came from a nation that had lost the war.

On this particular trip we were in Lucern, at the Hotel National, and so was the exiled King of Greece, with his wife and children and followers.

One day, not far from the hotel, sitting gallantly in the window of a toy shop, I had seen the dream to end all dreams in my young life: a horse, a wooden horse, a large wooden rocking horse. It was painted in luminous colors, with saddle and harness, and my heart went out to it at once. But Mil, trustee of the privy purse, would not hear of buying it for me. (How right she was!) The horse would have been far too large and heavy and cumbersome to ship back to Vienna, and besides it was outrageously expensive.

The sadness which this verdict inflicted on my heart is hard to describe. I quite literally went into a decline. That a family of recently-beaten Austro-Hungarians could not afford such a useless luxury was hard, nay impossible, for me to understand. Last but not least of Mil's objections to the horse was that I was certain to break my ruddy neck falling off it.

Inside me, desire and resentment went on smoldering, when lo and behold on a peaceful afternoon, right after lunch, while Mil was busy playing whist with some other ladies in a corner of the large hotel lobby, and nanny was probably occupied chatting with other nannies in another, I spied a friend, my only true faithful friend: the King of Greece. I lost no time and settled myself on his lap, which had of late become a comforting place for me. My mien must have been sorrowful, for he asked me what seemed to be the matter. More encouragement than that I did not need. I told him. The meanness of my grandmother came foremost. She would not buy me a simple toy, the beastly woman.

King George agreed that my grandmother—although he had to confess that she did not look it—must be an ogre indeed. But perhaps, he ventured, the situation might still be remedied. Where could this valiant horse be seen? I lost no time in telling him that as well. In a street not far from the hotel.

The King proceeded to take me by the hand, and together, like two thieves, totally unobserved by anyone, we snuck out of the hotel. Within a quarter of an hour the horse was mine. Of course, due to the size and shape of it, the horse would have to be delivered to the hotel later in the day. And so it was.

We were assembled upstairs in our sitting room— all of us, mothers and fathers, and aunts and uncles, and nannies, and me—when there was a knock on the door. Maria Herkenrot, my nanny, went to open, and there, seeming larger than a grand piano, stood a gigantic and mysterious box. I held my breath. But not for long. When the mystery box revealed the forbidden horse, the whole story was quickly squeezed out of me. Mil, who had immediately reverted to being an ogress, made her darkest face, thereby unleashing a Niagara of tears from me. But being a practical woman she paid my tears no heed at all. Instead, she marched right up to King George's apartment, knocked on his door, and gave him a piece of her mind. If, she said among many other things, she wanted her grandchild to break his limbs on this dangerous toy, she would have bought the silly horse herself. The horse was to be returned to the store forthwith.

There is a happy aftermath to this tale. Later on, back home in Vienna, I was given a lovely, delicious, ravishing giraffe. She was big enough to allow me to ride on her. But the giraffe, unlike the Swiss horse, was made of soft material. Nothing about her was lethal. Besides, she rolled on little metal wheels, whereas the horse had been made to rock. I loved my giraffe quite passionately. She was a lady, and therefore had to be made up with such lipstick and powder as my unsuspecting female relatives left sitting about. She also occasionally wore long veils, and on cold days a muffler around her neck. After all, giraffes having such long necks, I felt they must be quite sensitive to changes in temperature.

Ernst

Back in Vienna when I was about ready to enter Kindergarten, providence in one of its rare moments of magnanimity sent us the pearl of pearls, domestically speaking. His name was Ernst Puchtler. He was a Czech from the region of Eger. A footman in theory, but a poet, banker, playmate, chauffeur, cook, maid, philosopher, nursemaid, and trusted adviser in practice. Hardly twenty when he began his career with us, he had all the earmarks of unmistakable greatness, and was soon promoted from footman to butler. Later still, when we had moved to Paris, he became our majordomo.

No task that Ernst undertook was ever infested with awkwardness. Ernst could sew, cook, iron, swim, skate, paper walls, drive, and sing basso. Ernst took care of the dogs, played scat with Mil, and tucked me into bed. Ernst made Sachertorte as well as Frau Sacher, and his coffee was unrivaled. Ernst gave his opinion, though never unsolicited, on sundry matters of finance, art and industry—to us and to all our friends, who soon fell into the habit of seeking his advice on the most knotty problems.

Ernst traveled with us, fetched me from Kindergarten, and applied plaster to my bleeding knees. Ernst read one to sleep like nobody else, with "Treasure Island" and "The Last of the Mohicans." And Ernst could always be relied upon to think up new games for any children's party.

The living room of our apartment at the Hotel Ruhl in Nice, long our yearly winter quarters, had a large bay window. Ernst knew how to transform this with its heavy curtains, a chair or two, and a bit of string, into a regular Punch and Judy theater. Consequently, my children's parties were the hit of the Riviera.

There was not a thing that Ernst could not do. He was even known on one memorable occasion to retrieve a letter already posted in a public mailbox, when the sender, fickle Steph, had changed her mind about

Ernst—footman, butler, nursemaid,
philosopher, adviser and much more;
seated at left front with our staff in Biarritz.

sending it. No one ever found out whom Ernst had bribed—whether it was the mailman, or the President of the Republic.

One winter, Ernst, my governess, Miss Julia Richards, and I were exiled to the Pension Polonia on the Promenade des Anglais, in Nice, because it was suddenly deemed that too much living in luxury hostelries such as the Ruhl was bad for me. Ernst immediately knew how to make friends with Anna Pavlova, the celebrated Russian ballerina, who was also wintering at the Polonia.

Trust Ernst to know how to reach for the top.

Mil

In my grandmother Mil's order of priorities appearance ranked low—far behind serviceability and comfort. When seen one day, wearing one brown shoe and one black, this oversight was pointed out to her. But, without even troubling to look at her feet, she explained that it was no accident at all.

"Yes, I know," she said. "But the second brown one hurt me terribly."

Her indifference to what the world might think of her was impressive. Because of a mild case of claustrophobia, she was always rather reluctant to draw her bedroom curtains at night. When remonstrated by the rest of the family that "the people across the street can see you as you are undressing," Mil would merely point out, "Nothing is to prevent them from looking the other way."

Mil—wearing a pair of Mr. Gasar's painful shoes; Carlton Hotel Terrace, Cannes.

Mil and the Proletariat

During the time that people now call "the good old days," when Central Europe was suffering from inflation, Austria was having a revolution, the Balkans were starving, and street fighting was the most popular outdoor pastime, grandmother Mil was causing everyone many a headache. Especially in the matter of travel was her behavior whimsical. She flatly refused to acknowledge that the new post war world differed from the old world of yore. No longer was it possible to bespeak private railroad cars from Vienna to Budapest to attend the Hungarian Derby, as her late husband Hans had done on one or two occasions. Gone were the days of reserved trains in which she had ridden to the front during the war. Under the new republic, created after the Armistice of 1918, and headed by Steph's former catechism teacher, Monsignor Seipel, it took all one's patience and cunning to obtain a single third class ticket. Well-intentioned friends referred Mil to the word "adjustment," but in vain.

On several occasions Mil and the will of the people clashed. When, after her telephoned reservations and detailed dispatches to the stationmaster, she would arrive at her private compartment and find it besieged by a rabble of snickering plebians, obviously ready for a brawl, the stage was set for fireworks.

Planting herself with porters and luggage in the exact center of the passage, thereby obstructing all further traffic, she would summon the conductor and demand in no uncertain terms that "these common people" be immediately ejected. As a result of this ill-timed insistence on fading constitutional rights, she was all but lynched on several occasions. Fortunately she was quite capable of lynching right back, and when the law failed to acquit itself of its duty, she would take it into her own capable hands. She did this with considerable alacrity, and usually succeeded in making the trip so miserable for the misguided proletarians that they were finally only too willing to relinquish the dubious pleasure of our company. One after the other they would traipse off ignominiously bruised, battered and beaten, while Mil sat triumphant in her hard-earned privacy.

The means she employed to accomplish this were manifold. One of the favorite tricks from her repertoire was to suddenly become very grand maternal. Opening a tin of condensed milk, without which she considered it imprudent to travel, and under the feeble pretense of feeding me, the infant, she would spill a goodly portion of its gooey content, accompanied by profuse hypocritical apologies, on those unfortunate to be seated close to her.

"How this could have happened I'm sure I don't know," she would say in the tones of a cherub. Amazed by her own actions, she never knew how deviltries of her own instigation had come about. At other times she would unravel a well-seasoned camembert cheese, for which there was no excuse whatsoever. (Our household was well stocked with a variety of cheeses supplied by Henry of Mecklenburg, Prince Consort of the Queen of Holland, Wilhelmina, with whom Steph did a lot of mountain climbing in Switzerland. Consequently, Mil was never short of traveling ammunition.)

Nor was Mil above creating havoc by "accidentally" locking passengers in or out of their compartments, by means of her vast assortment of pass keys.

As far as my own participation went—well rehearsed and loudly prompted—it was out of the question that I be taken to the nearest loo when my bladder so demanded.

"Far too dirty," was Mil's virdict. She simply would not hear of it. All this had to be performed right there in the compartment under the eyes and noses of all present, into a gold and silver goblet engraved with the family crest. The content was thereupon emptied out the window. If it so chanced, as it mostly did, that the wind blew some of this princely uric acid back on the clothes of the fellow travelers, Mil would wave that aside with a chemical fallacy: "'Tis only water," she would say.

By the time all these legerdemains had been performed we usually had the compartment to ourselves.

On one occasion, however, Mil met with obdurate resistance. This happened on an unforgettable journey from Salzburg to Vienna. Mil, Steph, Pop, my nurse Maria Herkenrot, one of my uncles, footman Ernst, our maid Louise Mainz, several dogs, and I were occupying the better part of a coach, short of the portion alloted to freight. What with Mil's copious picnic baskets, Steph's veritable library of reading material, and Pop and my uncle's rifles, the cubic space was well taken care of.

Mil, Nanny, the dogs and I were supposed to have one of those European oddities, a half-compartment to ourselves; or so proclaimed the large vermillion letters, "Reserviert Privat," on the glass door. But a gentleman of good appearance and unusual strength of character was already installed in the compartment when we arrived, and, vexatiously, nothing could dislodge him. His good appearance we soon took care of, but his staying power we were unable to affect. One of the dogs made a meal of his kid gloves while shedding long skye terrier hairs on his overcoat. This our imper-turbable stranger either did not see, or chose to ignore. His muffler was used by Maria in a moment of aberration to wipe some carbonated water that Mil had carelessly spilled on his hat.

At this point the taciturn stranger spoke his first words. They were discouraging, for he said, "Think nothing of it."

As for the opening and closing of windows, usually a moot point of contention, it seemed not to affect him at all. He was equally agreeable to all our desires regarding temperature; suffocating one minute, blown off his feet the next. Such patience was worthy of an early Christian martyr. It irritated us to distraction. Who wants a Saint for a traveling companion? Mil tried all her bag of proven tricks. Even I was very loyal to the cause: being sick right on his lap, then accidently hitting his right eye with a teddy bear. But my cooperation was wasted. Nothing could disturb his even tenor. We arrived in Vienna worn out and defeated. In fact, we were the first to leave the scene of our own shambles, for Mil had a way of leaning out compartment windows and gleaning every available porter.

The last we saw of Mr. Imperturbable, as we looked back over our shoulders, he was still sitting quietly where we had found him in Salzburg—smiling the enigmatic smile of a Mona Lisa. But a Mona Lisa much the worse for wear, whom Leonardo would scarcely have painted.

Gifts of love

I discovered my penchant for the made-to-order early in life. "Store boughten" presents were all right in their way, but one's deeper feelings were better expressed, especially at Christmas, by something unique and handmade.

One holiday gift of love to my father was to wash all his cigarette holders with strong soap and water. It speaks volumes for his patience that he did not apply his riding whip to my backside.

Ernst, who also ranked high in my esteem, was treated to a somewhat similar endearment. I spent many weeks before Christmas collecting cigarette stubs from all the ashtrays and, carefully removing the paper, trimming off the burnt edges. With a flourish and in a large tote bag adorned with a bow, I presented Ernest my collection of loose tobacco. His brave smile and holiday hug convinced me that I had hit on exactly the right present.

On the other hand, my first girl friend, Ilse, showed none of Ernst's tender understanding. Borrowing the unloaded family Kodak, I asked her to pose for me. Click went the shutter. The following day I cut an unlikely but pretty picture from some magazine, and gave it to her as a personalized snapshot. Being no dummy, she tore up the picture, bopped me on the head with her doll, and walked off in a huff.

The fanciest present of all was reserved for Steph. For her benefit I wrote a whole book. All five pages of it. I still have it. She kept it all her life and I inherited it. My book was a novel. I illustrated it myself. Since my spelling was dubious, the original manuscript was corrected by Ernst, a much better speller than I. He then carried the magnum opus to a typist, and even had it bound in red morocco leather, paying for it out of his wages. Greater love hath no footman.

My novel began with the immortal words, "In winter, when it gets cold in Vienna, one travels to the Riviera." Oh, innocent little rich boy!

Another frequent beneficiary of my largesse was Miss Richards, my governess. Once, during a hike in the mountains near St. Gilgen, while exploring a cave, I came upon an old boot. Because of its size, shape, and other aspects, this boot seemed very mysterious. It must surely have belonged to a fierce pirate with a black patch over one eye. Why a sea pirate should have chosen the mountains of Austria in which to lose one of his boots did not disturb me. My being deep into reading "Treasure Island" at the time may have had something to do with it.

Just as Jesus was quite obviously Austrian, in spite of all that nonsense about Nazareth and Bethlehem. He was, I felt quite certain, born in Vienna on a very cold winter night. Wasn't "Silent Night" always sung while icicles hung outside the windows?

But back to the Austrian pirate's boot. It had, no doubt about it, great historical value. Any museum in its right mind would covet it. Therefore, it was a worthy object to give as a present. Miss Richards, whom I dearly loved, was the recipient. She accepted it with ladylike equanimity. Since I cannot recall her keeping it for long, she must have passed it on to the Metropolitan Museum in New York, or possibly the Louvre.

Even our dogs did not escape my generosities. It was a terrible injustice, I felt, that they must always walk on their own four legs. So I treated them to relaxing rides in a small wooden cart, for which I was the horse. The cart was decked out with cushions and lap rugs to make it more comfortable, for I loved the dogs and wanted them to ride at ease. As compensation for the ardours of these journeys, usually along a passage that led from my nursery to the bathroom on one side, and the linen room on the other, the cart also held chocolate cake and bowls of refreshing water. All our dogs were tea-totalers.

I was deeply hurt when our dogs seemed to lack a spirit of cooperation, and fell back on a more responsive playmate—my stuffed giraffe. Here the roles were somewhat reversed. I was no longer a horse, but a cavalier. I rode her astride. Yes, she was a she. Her lips, to accentuate her femininity, were periodically reddened with some of Steph's more expensive lipsticks, and she wore veils and jewels—the latter courtesy of Mil's costume jewelry box. She was by far the most graterful recipient of my magnanimities. I loved her passionately. In retrospect, I think I still do.

A small mistake

My early life was replete with uncles and aunts and great uncles and great aunts of every description. Great Aunt Rosa was one of my favorites. When she came to visit us in winter, wearing an astrakhan coat with snowflakes clinging to her collar, we could smell the good snow on fur as we embraced her.

It was Great Aunt Rosa who decided one day that she would take me to the theater to a real play, an operetta, and for the evening performance! I had been to the opera fairly often, but only in the afternoon, and only for ballet performances. Certain ballets such as Coppelia were deemed suitable for children. We had a box, and living plum across from the Vienna State Opera as we did, it was a simple matter to transfer me from my nursery to our box. Our cook, Katie, and Ernst, and of course my governess, were also allowed to slip in and out for a short while. It was, in fact, quite a family affair. But Great Aunt Rosa's invitation ranked far above that. An evening performance! What an event! She even threw in an invitation to dinner beforehand, at the Imperial Hotel, because it was close to the theater.

I was decked out in my best finery and Great Aunt Rosa came to fetch me and we walked to the Imperial where she was well known, because she met Mil there almost every night for a game of whist. After dinner, as we were crossing the lobby toward the front door, I espied two people I knew who were just entering through the revolving door. They were Sir Woodman and Lady Burbridge, at that time owners of Harrod's, London's select department store. They were friends of my family. I went forward to greet them, and did the right thing as I had been taught, but in the excitement of this red letter evening it came out wrong. I energetically shook the hand of Lady Burbridge, and deposed a delicate kiss on the hairy fingers of Sir Woodman.

The Magyar blood that flows in my veins

I had six grandparents. How so? Because my paternal grandfather married twice, as did my maternal grandmother. On Pop's side, Countess Franziska Esteházy de Galantha was grandmother number one, followed by stepgrandmother Countess Majlath.

Mil, for her part, had Dr. Johannes Richter as her number one, and Baron Kálman Negyessy de Szepessy as her number two. Of these six grandparents, four were Hungarian and only two Austrian.

As for Pop (which he did not know I called him behind his back), after Steph divorced him he married Countess Dessewffy, born Countess Ella Bátthyány. Another Hungarian. Aunt Ella, as I called my step-mother, had three sons by her first marriage—my step-stepbrothers, three more Hungarians. It all boils down to this: despite my Vienna birth and German name, we were top-heavy with Hungarians.

F.H. in Hungarian
"disz Magyar"
nobleman's
uniform.

Pop, since we are speaking of him, was, during my school years, president of the Hungarian Aviation Company. Hungary had only one. The engines of our aeroplanes were bought in Holland from the Fokker Company, which gave Pop occasion to travel to Amsterdam rather frequently. So there we were, the three of us, my divorced parents and I, in the land of tulips and windmills. We had put up at the Hotel des Indes in the Hague. The day after our arrival Pop had a meeting scheduled at the Amsterdam airport with some gentlemen from the Fokker Company.

Mostyn, our chauffeur for the English cars, drove us to the airport in Steph's cabriolet Rolls-Royce. I think that on that occasion she had a sky-blue-with-black-trim whopper of a car. In Holland, a country of understatements, the car became surrounded by a crowd of gapers wherever it was parked. We dropped Steph at the Amstel Hotel and continued—Pop, Mostyn and I—toward the airport.

"Be back at five in time for tea," Steph called over her shoulder. "I shall meet you here on the terrace of the hotel." It was high summer and warm and sunny and lovely.

When we reached the airport, Pop had one predominant wish: to get rid of me as quickly as possible in order to devote his thinking to matters of business. He entrusted me to a pilot who happened to have some time on his hands, with instructions to fly me around for an hour or so and then bring me back—alive, if possible.

It was the first time I had been up in a plane. The pilot, a sturdy young Dutchman, was as pleased with me as a passenger as I was with him as a pilot. He decided to show me everything a plane could do, from spins and rolls to looping the loop. I am still surprised when I recall the event that the small machine did not come apart at the seams. It was wonderful!

But of course, what with my flying all over the ether, and Pop's lengthy business discussion, we were almost an hour late in returning to the Amstel hotel. Steph, who was just about the most impatient person on earth, could be seen in the distance, stalking the terrace overlooking the Amstel River, like a tigress in the zoo.

Steph's first words were addressed to poor Pop. "One must hail from the Balkans to keep a woman waiting for over an hour." (Not true. We were late, but not over an hour.) In moments of high tension she always became very Viennese, and Budapest together with all the Balkans became outposts of civilization. She then turned to me and said, "Don't stand there grinning like an idiot. And don't think I don't know where you have been the last hour!"

Steph and Pop, who had been divorced about ten years, were at that time toying with the notion of getting married again. But finally they dropped this project out of their decent feelings toward Aunt Ella, whom both genuinely liked and did not want to hurt. None the less, they had many trysts of which they informed no one, and which only came to light when one chanced upon snapshots of them together taken in such different places as Lake Balaton or Berlin, where they were guests of Crown Prince Wilhelm in Potsdam.

Of all this, of course, Ella knew nothing. Whenever Steph arrived in Budapest, which was often, because His Highness Admiral Horthy, Regent of Hungary, frequently called her for advice, she would ring up Ella at once.

"I am here. Can you have lunch with me tomorrow, here at the Ritz? But without Franzi (my father). We don't want to act as a harem to him."

For my part, I was terribly fond of Aunt Ella. And she in turn showered kindness on me. I was the youngest of her four boys, and the child she had not had with Pop. My room in Pop's house in Budapest, at Ilona Utca 9, she had decorated—in impeccable taste. She and I both had weaknesses for the combination of red and white, the Hohenlohe colors. My bathroom was all red and white. Even the toilet seat was lacquered red, a real rarity in those days. Unfortunately, my Hungarian was way under par and I was often sent for long periods to my step-grandfather to Borsod Megye, to beat the language into my skull. But it was uphill work, and I still speak only kitchen Hungarian.

Crown Prince Wilhelm

The case of the poisoned coffee

All her life Mil hovered in a precarious state of truce with first her own and later with her daughter's servants; a state best described as an armed peace. In the Vienna days she never allowed our superlative cook, Katie, to do the daily shopping. Mil considered that only her own judgment in the matter of freshness and quality was valid. Also, she could not bring herself to trust Katie with the household money.

Katie, who was always dressed in darkest black, as though in mourning for the late Queen Victoria's Consort, knew to a nicety what went on in Mil's suspicious mind. She showed her contempt for such shenanigans by swishing the small train with which all her somber garments were adorned.

Mil set out for the Naschmarkt bright and early each day, "so as not to get other people's leftovers," clutching her reticule in one hand and a shopping list that she never consulted in the other. A few steps behind followed one of the kitchen maids, whose duty it was to carry an assortment of nets and baskets.

Mil's scrutiny, through a tortise-shell lorgnette attached to her bodice by a black ribbon, was critical and severe. The quality of butter was often a matter of special vexation. It seldom met with her complete approval. Her surreptitious dipping of an exploratory finger into it did little to arouse the sympathy of the dairywomen selling it.

Never under any circumstances did she purchase more than that day's supplies, as anything left over from one day to the next was considered a major health hazard. Therein she was probably right, since refrigeration then was not what it is today.

In Paris, the status quo which hung uneasily between Mil and the servants became more distant and formalized. Paul, our autocratic French chef, did not look kindly on anyone, staff or masters alike, invading his kitchen. Only Marie, the scullery maid, whom we suspected of being Paul's mistress, was allowed in this off-limits zone. It was, after all, where she was earning her living. What Paul had figuratively roped off was tacitly understood to include not only the kitchen itself but also the pantry, the larder, the still room, and the silver vault. Mil could penetrate only as far as the butler's pantry, far removed from Paul's sphere of influence. She accepted this state of affairs grudgingly. Her morning, afternoon and evening coffees were brewed for her in that pantry by Ernst, whom we had brought with us from Vienna. Leaving him behind would have been unthinkable, as he was part of the family.

In the dramatic love-hate relationship which existed between them, seldom to be found outside the plays of Ibsen or Aristophanes, Mil periodically accused Ernst of using stagnant water, of experimenting with lesser brands of coffee than those which found their way into Steph's quarters, and much, much more. As poor, devoted Ernst ground fresh coffee by hand for every cup in the sort of machine that has since completely disappeared from even the best run households, this was indeed unfair.

One morning, Steph was lying in her lovely bed in the sunny bedroom of her Paris apartment and enjoying breakfast, a Skye terrier or two at her feet hoping for small donations. Suddenly, Ernst appeared at the door and announced, "Two gentlemen from the criminal police are in the hall and wish to speak to Your Highness."

Steph thereupon choked on a croissant, but had enough breath left to say, "From the criminal police?"

"Yes, so these gentlemen said."

What incredible things could happen in this strange city of Paris, so different from her native Vienna. Steph put on a dressing gown and went into the hall. There the police inspectors explained that they had come "Dans l'affaire des poisons."

"The matter of the poisoning? What poisoning? Who was poisoned?"

"But Madame," said one of the officers, "you have, after all, sent some coffee to be analyzed for traces of poison! In France such an action must immediately be reported to the criminal police."

A gleam of understanding came into Steph's eyes. Bidding the inspectors to wait in the lobby, she disappeared like an arrow in the direction of Mil's bedroom, where the latter was also breakfasting.

"Mother," she said, in a voice which ruthlessly

shook the culprit, "did you send some coffee to a laboratory to be analyzed for poison?"

"Yes I did. Yesterday's coffee. I sent my maid, right after breakfast."

"What on earth for?"

"Because I think it was poisoned. It tasted funny."

"But Ernst makes your coffee himself!"

"That's just it. I think he's poisoning me."

"But you can't really mean that! Anyway, how do you know what poison tastes like?"

"I should think much like my coffee did yesterday morning," answered Mil.

A few days later, a somewhat peeved Mil was heard to say, "I think Ernst is avoiding me."

"Are you surprised?" asked Steph. "You called him a thief last month and a murderer this month."

"But I did nothing of the sort. I only said that he stole my emerald ring."

"Well, isn't that being a thief?"

"Of course not. I found it later on, under some papers in my desk drawer. So obviously he didn't take it after all. I told him so afterward. As for the coffee, it has much improved. He gets so upset over trifles."

Marthe Capitaine

For many years after we had moved to Paris, a faithful soul by the name of Marthe Capitaine filled our several homes in France with songs, and the linen room with the clatter of her sewing machine. The songs were culled for the most part straight off the streets of Montmartre, or the popular music halls.

Marthe Capitaine was French, a true "Titi Parisienne." She was unmarried and of indeterminate age, always cheerful, very ugly, and good as gold. She was invariably dressed in frivolous adaptations of the current mode. Her skirts were worn well above the knees during the jazzy twenties, and dramatically long during the depression thirties. She had her meals in the servants' hall and was, thank God, totally impervious to the sometimes cruel jibes of our staff, who were given to teasing her.

Mademoiselle Capitaine—never known by her Christian name in those less democratic days—followed us from Paris to Nice, from Nice to Monte Carlo, from Monte Carlo to Biarritz, then back to Paris. Everywhere we owned, leased or rented houses, villas and apartments, she was enthroned in the linen room.

She worked and sang and gossiped from morning 'til night while mending sheets, darning the footmen's socks, repairing towels and aprons, cutting out burnt edges of dishrags, lengthening or shortening sleeves and hemlines, and whipping up "little black dresses" for Mil.

Sometimes she was also called upon to take in, or let out (more often the latter), a seam or waistband belonging to Steph, or deal with a precious piece of Valenciennes lace, or crepe de Chine. Occasionally she was asked to extend the life span of one of Steph's "Coupe Recamier" bras. These bras required endless adjustments according to whether their owner was winning or losing the battle of the bulge. Oh healthy Viennese appetite! Added to this came the circumstance that only a very few of the bras became Steph's favorites, while others, ordered, paid for but never worn, were relegated to the back of her closet.

Steph's bras were a story onto themselves. They were custom made by the Maison Cadolle on the rue Cambon. Despite that, only one in ten met with her approval. Consequently, while nine were banished, the tenth reached a ripe old age—worn, cherished, and mended over and over again.

One afternoon in Cannes at the Carlton Hotel where we stayed, Steph became exasperated that one of the bras she intended to wear was completely worn from battle fatigue. She flung the ungrateful garment across the room and retired to her bathroom. Steph's bathrooms, wherever she happened to be, were chambers of great predilection to her. She spent a goodly portion of her days in them, soaking, reading, meditating, composing newspaper articles, writing memos, telephoning, and even receiving the more intimate female members of her family and friends.

On this particular day when she emerged from the bathroom she had forgotten the offending bra and had dressed.

Later in the afternoon she was sitting at a table in the Casino when it slowly became apparent to her that people were observing her rather strangely. She could not fathom what this was all about until she returned to her apartment at the Carlton. It then became abundantly clear. She had spent the entire afternoon in front of hundreds of people wearing nothing at all under a sheer mousseline dress. She had forgotten to put on a bra, and those were not yet the days of see-through blouses.

This was one time when Mademoiselle Capitaine was not at fault. Marthe's talents were multilateral, although no one could have accused her of being a grade A seamstress. She leaned more to speed than fidelity. Mil, who had her copy some of Steph's high fashion creations, would occasionally come apart at the seams in the middle of a tea party, or while getting in or out of a taxi.

On a red letter day one of Mil's sleeves fell off in the Palm Beach Casino at Cannes as she was reaching for some chips on the table. This was doubly memorable for the occasion was indubitably a joyous one. She had just won. Such an unbelievable rarity! Fortunately, Mil was not one to be embarrassed by an incident of so trivial a nature. She simply rose above it, pocketed the offending sleeve along with her winnings, and went right on gambling. Both sleeve and loot were stuffed into her handbag while she dared anyone to titter.

On another memorable occasion, Mil's skirt dropped off in mid Champs Elysées. She was equal to the situation. Stepping out of it with the dexterity of a Russian ballerina, as if this happened to her every day (and it must be admitted that it quite frequently did), she hung it over her arm, slipped into an overcoat that she was providentially carrying, and went on her way.

We who were accompanying her, three spotty-faced school chums and myself, whom she was treating to a film matinée at the Colisée Cinema, took it less stoically. To put it mildly, we thought we would sink through the pavement in embarrassment. The more so as Mil at that point in her life was given to wearing long flannel underwear of the type that went out of fashion on the day of Queen Victoria's funeral. These knickers, although they at least had the grace of not being red, belonged quite definitely in a book of illustrations for homely virtues. Only the gradual shortening of women's dresses made Mil finally abandon them.

It was one of the surprising sides of Mil's character that she looked so plain and unpretentious, but when you scratched the surface you found that everything that went into the making of this low profile image was hellishly expensive. The antedeluvian knickers were in fact made to measure for her by the ultra-conservative Braun & Co. of Vienna, Karlsbad, Munich, New York and Palm Beach. They cost a mint.

When people knew her better, they began to notice things about this simple, unmade-up, down-to-earth woman which surprised them. Her never-changing low-heeled shoes were a prime example. They were handmade by Monsieur Gasar, a Czech. He called on her in the evenings after his regular working hours, for she would never go to him. Her equally no-nonsense handbags may have been Steph's hand-me-downs, but they hailed mostly from Cartier.

A little diamond brooch in the shape of a tree, and another one shaped like a cross-legged Buddha, were signed Van Cleef & Arpels.

Her favorite platitude was, "The smallest room in the best hotel is preferable to a suite in a second-rate one."

This was closely followed by, "It is essential for a woman to have one good fur coat."

Where the money for the best hotel and the fur coat was to come from lay beyond her sphere of interest.

Marthe Capitaine, who had to whip up dresses to be worn under the fur coats, lived on the Boulevard Richard Lenoir, near the Place de la Republique, which was quite a long way from our house. This never prevented her from being on time for work, come snow or high water. Perhaps she would not have been such a slapdash seamstress if she had been given a little more time to perfect her copies. But Mil was an impatient woman, always needing her clothes made with the speed of lightning.

Marthe's songs sprang forth from lips painted in a

scarlet cupid's bow, covering very crooked teeth. Her hair was shingled in an Eton crop, save for two spit curls rather dashingly Spanish. Rings were a passion with her. She wore one on practically every finger short of the thumbs. The cloche hats she favored were worn so low over her eyes that she must have been a menace to other pedestrians. She preferred dresses in bright colors and shiny materials with sashes worn low, almost meeting the hemline. The term "mini skirt" may not yet have been invented, but the short, short skirt certainly had. Finally, her shoes! Their Louis XV heels could only be described as giddy.

But the songs I learned by listening to her trill away have remained engraven in my memory to this day. They have also, not infrequently, cheered me up in bleak moments of my existence.

Dear Mademoiselle Capitaine—so gay, so frivolous, so loyal, despite the meager assets with which Fate had endowed her!

Biarritz

We had a villa in Biarritz, the villa Goncer, in a part of
that town which bears the unlikely name of "La
Négresse." The villa Goncer, a late Victorian-type
building, was very large, very ugly, and very comfortable.
I was supremely happy there. It had, among many other
pleasant features, a life-size doll house, the best of my
latest Christmas presents, which had been folded and
transported from Paris, and re-erected by the side of
our tennis court. This doll house, fully furnished, could
hold eleven of my gang, if we squeezed into it like
sardines.

Of all the children at the Chiberta Country Club,
my special cronies were the three sons of Marie-Pilar,
Marquise de Bethulia, and the two sons of Angustia,
Marquise de San Carlos. Since in Spain the children of
the aristocracy bear different names from those of their
parents, the Bethulia offspring were called Zulueta,
and the San Carlos offspring de Pedroso. We were all
between eight and eleven years old, with me at the
lower end of the scale—which didn't prevent me from
being the gang leader. Since it took very little to amuse
us, the games I thought up were on the simple side. On
rainy days we stayed in the house where one of the
seldom used guest rooms had become our headquarters.
It was a large, old-fashioned room with an enormous

oak bed in the middle. Both bed and room always smelled musty. Our favorite game was playing kings. An assortment of chamber pots which we had garnered from other rooms served as crowns. Since each one of us had a chamber pot on his head we were all, most democratically, equal kings. If a long piece of some fluffy material (purloined from Mademoiselle Capitaine's sewing machine) was attached to the handle, the "crown" belonged to the queen—except that none

Biarritz—the three Counts Zulueta in front;
putting chamber pots on our heads
was a favorite indoor game.

of us ever wanted to be queen. Polo, our eleven-year-old, spotty-faced groom, who joined our games if not otherwise engaged running errands for the family, would often be forced into this role. With the adorned chamber pot on his head he made a very adequate if spotty-faced queen.

On sunny days our intellectual games took us outside. The big favorite among all our pastimes was lurking in the vicinity of the garage, in the hope that Gaston would repair to the kitchen quarters where we knew that he maintained a flirtation with the kitchen maid, Marie. Since we also suspected Marie of being the lady love of Paul, our chef, Gaston had uphill work to do to push his advantage. And uphill work takes time. Gaston also, quite frequently, left the car keys of the Chenard & Walker on the dashboard. And this is what we were waiting for. No sooner had Gaston turned his back than we jumped in the car. Fortunately, the garage was situated far from the main house, so no one heard us starting up the engine. The chosen driver was I, since Gaston himself had taught me the rudiments of driving when I was seven, sitting on his lap. Still, even with this experience behind me, my driving was shaky. Turning corners posed especially great problems, as our sporty Chenard & Walker was no easier to handle than an army tank. The corners of our lawns got the worst of it, and whenever the gardner or one of his aides caught us ruining his lawns he came after us with a pitchfork.

We all met up again after the war. The de Pedroso

boys and I in Philadelphia, the Zuluetas and I in Manila. The war, in fact, was not yet quite over, and I arrived in the Phillipines with the United States Army. The youngest Zulueta had married shortly before the outbreak of hostilities, and his wife had just borne him his first child when the Japanese army invaded Manila. Nipponese soldiers were going from house to house, planting bayonettes in everything that moved. One morning they reached the Zulueta villa on the outskirts of Manila. Fortunately, young Countess Zulueta did not lose her head. She lay down on top of her baby and played dead, hoping to God the child would not cry. By a miracle it didn't, and taking her for a corpse, the soldiers walked right by her. The days of the kingly chamber pots were truly far behind us.

Anna

Anna was Steph's lady's maid. I loved her very much, and she loved me just as much in return. In the period when I was too big for a governess, but not big enough to be allowed to run about the streets alone, it became Anna's side duty to go out with me, when her other work allowed it. We understood each other admirably, although Anna was addicted to deep sighs, and it was only after having sighed deeply several times, to show how overworked she was, that she would consent to go out into the streets with me. Naturally, the ironing and brushing, and sewing, and threading pink silk ribbons through bed pillows, and removing black stains from satin evening slippers which had suffered ill treatment during Charleston dancing—all this had to come first. But once I had managed to entice her away from her other duties and we were out on our own, she became quite jovial.

In Deauville we were given a small sum of money every afternoon, to allow us to consume two ices and two pastries on the terrace of the casino. To say that I was a hotel, casino and luxury palace brat is putting it mildly. I knew the ins and outs of every five-star establishment in Europe.

When, also in Deauville, Anna sometimes accompanied me to the beach of an early morning, we would occasionally bump into Mil, on her way home from a night's gambling at the casino. She was a very modest but inveterate gambler. Not infrequently she would be walking along arm-in-arm with the Shah of Persia—the one just before the Pahlevis, who, it was said, had lost both his money and his throne for the beautiful eyes of dancer Gaby Deslys. Their days were ending. Ours began.

In Naples I once succeeded in luring poor, plump Anna into a sidecar-taxi. In those years, only Italy had such contraptions. As the chauffeur would not let me straddle the motorbike behind him, I had to squeeze myself into the sidecar more on top of Anna than beside her. But whoever has not ridden over the bumpy pavements of Naples in a sidecar-taxi has not lived life to its fullest.

Anna was, as already mentioned, more Catholic than the Pope and more royalist than a King, and also very anti-Semitic. Her hair was worn combed straight back, giving her a severe appearance. No one would have suspected her kind heart under that surface—for those she liked.

One late afternoon at the Hotel Royal in Deauville, someone knocked on Steph's sitting room door. Steph herself had not yet come home from her afternoon occupations. Anna, who was laying out the evening clothes in the bedroom, put on her grumpiest face and went to open the door. Outside stood Baron Maurice de Rothschild, whom Anna had never been able to tolerate.

"We are not at home," said Anna, and made ready

to shut the door in the portly Baron's face. But Maurice de Rothschild was too quick for her. He slipped very nimbly past her bosom into the sitting room and settled himself in a large armchair.

"Then I shall wait," he said, thus dismissing Anna, who shrugged her shoulders and returned to her work in the bedroom. But after awhile Baron Maurice got bored, sitting there all alone. He got up and entered the bedroom, where Anna had just finished with her last touches: the evening bag, the shoes, the bra, the handkerchief. The Baron, who thought that standing was a poor occupation, was just about to let his ample posterior down on the bed. Not only that, but right on top of a small chinchilla evening cape! Chinchilla! The most fragile of all furs! This, was too much for Anna. She took Baron de Rothschild by the lapels and boldly pushed him out the apartment door.

Another day, this time at Claridge's in London, Anna was standing guard while her mistress took a little nap. There was a knock on the door. Outside stood a man, and Anna did not trouble to ask who he was.

"We are resting and cannot be disturbed," she announced. The man turned his heels and walked away very peaceably.

When Steph awoke a little later on, Anna informed her of the visitor.

"What did he look like?"

"Like two profiles stuck together."

"Oh my God, that was the King of Spain. I was supposed to have tea with him!"

My uncle the Bishop

The twenties were at their roaringest, and in chic and frivolous Budapest there was a Hotel Ritz, also known as the Dunapalota, which means Danube Palace in Hungarian. On the terrace of this hotel, which overlooked the river and also the Var, the old city on the other shore, there was a *thé dansant* every afternoon throughout the summer. This was customary at the time in all major luxury hotels all over Europe and elsewhere.

On one such afternoon two elderly ladies of the highest Hungarian aristocracy were sitting at their table, looking over the scene with their lorgnettes, while sipping their tea in delicate Heerend porcelain china cups. Lorgnettes were de rigueur at that time. Suddenly the lorgnette of one of the ladies began trembling in her hand.

"My dear," she said to her companion, "do look over there. Isn't that Bishop Hohenlohe dancing the tango?"

Bishop Hohenlohe it was.

To explain this incident fully and show my poor uncle in a slightly better light, let me add that soon thereafter he married his tango partner, the pretty and perfectly respectable Mademoiselle Edith de Gaspar, who bore him three children—my cousins, the very ones who now live in Buenos Aires. Of course the scandal was tremendous. Not only did he have to leave the Catholic church, but he also had to leave Hungary for good and ever.

Enghien

I loved my grandmother Mil with all my heart, and with all, in spite of all, because of all, her weaknesses. Gambling was one of the major ones. She was, after all, my only grandmother. Grandmother Estehązy, on father's side, had died before my birth. It is sad that someone who had six grandparents should have known only one of them.

One of Mil's best traits was her capacity for laughter. She played bridge, and chess, and whist, and Mah Jong, and écarté, and baccarat, and chemin de fer. And seldom did she come out winning. But none of this kept her from laughing.

When I was eleven or thereabouts, my five-year-older cousin Bertie, who lived in Berlin, came to visit us in Paris. He was given my bedroom, since I was away at school, and Mil proceeded to show him Paris from top to bottom. Bertie, toward whom Mil always felt slightly guilty since she saw so much less of him, was taken to the Louvre and the Eiffel Tower, and the Sacré Coeur, and Versailles, and goodness knows what all else. But on the seventh day, like Our Lord when He had finished creating the world, Mil felt that a little respite was in order.

"Tomorrow afternoon," she told Bertie, "I shall take you to Enghien."

"Enghien-les-Bains, as I think it is called by its full name, is a delightful small resort very close to Paris, with a charming casino by the side of a miniature lake. During the Belle Epoque the Enghien Casino was a favorite of the beau monde who drove there in their high-slung automobiles.

When Mil and Bertie arrived in Enghien, she advised him thus:

"Why don't you rent yourself a rowboat there on the lake?" As she said it, she handed him some French money. "At seven-thirty, be in the lobby of the casino. I shall take you to dinner here. Food in all casinos is very good. It's a way they have of luring gamblers."

Thus dismissed, Bertie did as he was told, while his grandma disappeared into the entrails of the casino.

Good boy as he was, Bertie spent his afternoon in healthy pursuits, and at the given hour, full of invigorating fresh air, he made for the casino lobby. As yet, Mil was nowhere to be seen. Bertie sat in a chair with good visibility of the gaming room entrance, and began to wait. He waited and waited, and waited some more. Just as he was beginning to have doubts that he would ever clap eyes on her again, she appeared—and a sorry sight she was. Her chic cloche hat sat askew. Her dress seemed rumpled, her stance was forlorn, and her handbag (signed Cartier; a hand-me-down of her daughter's) looked frighteningly flat.

"Grandmama," said Bertie, who had not yet gotten into the stride of calling her Mil, "whatever happened to you? You look so odd."

"Those thieves," replied the odd-looking one. "I had such a good winning streak. In the beginning, that is. But then they changed the croupier. They do that all the time, you know, when they see that someone is in a winning streak." Bertie said he understood, but of course he didn't.

"This new man," Mil continued, "had a totally different way of throwing the ball into the roulette. This changes everything, you must know. I lost all my winnings, and a little more on top of that."

"Never mind," said Bertie. "You will feel much better after dinner, you'll see."

"Dinner?" said Mil, as though she had never heard the word before and took it for a sound out of Mongolia. "I'm afraid you didn't quite understand me. When I said I had lost everything, I meant everything. There won't be any money for dinner."

But at that moment a flash of genius came to her rescue. "You know," she said, "I have an idea. When people have won at the tables they are always ridiculously generous. Really quite vulgar. You must go to the men's room at once, where there is sure to be a plate with many ill-deserved tips. Pocket them and bring them to me. After all, the casino surely owes me a dinner."

Mil's logic was often totally illogical. Meanwhile, Bertie had perceptibly paled. But he was a staunch supporter of the family, so he trotted off to the gentlemen's loo, and there, while no one was looking, emptied the plate of vulgar tips. After all, the casino owed them two dinners. Grandma had said so. With this ill-gotten loot they ate two pairs of sausages, while standing up across the street from the casino.

And how did they get home to Paris? Quite simply. In Stephanie's borrowed Hispano-Suiza—with chauffeur if you please. After all, "noblesse oblige."

Mr. Gasar and the painful shoes

Mr. Gasar was Mil's shoemaker. And a very good shoemaker he was. He made all of Mil's shoes during the seven years we lived in Paris. Which comes to say that he really only made one pair of shoes—in black, in brown, and in silk for evening wear—as all her life Mil never varied the model. Mil had very ugly feet and couldn't have cared less. But her feet were also deformed and sensitive, which grieved her a great deal. In her childhood, one of the youngest of ten children, her parents, who had to be parsimonious with such a large brood, made her wear all the hand-me-downs of her older sisters. These shoes were invariably too small, too tight, too short, but never to her size. In consequence, her poor feet had been irremediably deformed. Mr. Gasar understood this, and being such a fine shoemaker did what he could to cause her the minimum of pain.

Mr. Gasar always came to our apartment, and always in the evening as we were finishing dinner. If he came early, Ernst, who was a big crony as well as a compatriot of his—both were from Czechoslovakia—was told to give Mr. Gasar a little glass of Schnapps in the pantry while he waited.

The shoe trials, in the fullest sense of the word, took place in the dining room, with Mr. Gasar sitting at Mil's feet, surrounded by all his boxes. "Mr. Gasar," she'd say, "these new shoes hurt me terribly, especially here over the toes, on the left. You have used a much harder leather than usual."

"Gracious lady," he'd reply—being Czech he spoke a special jargon of his own—"Gracious lady, I have used the same soft leather as I used last time and all the times before in the seven years I have made shoes for you."

"I can't believe that, Mr. Gasar. This leather seems terribly hard to me. Much harder than ever before. I can't wear these shoes like that. You must soften them considerably."

"These shoes are made of the same fine leather as the brown ones you like so much, and which are full of holes, you have worn them so much, and I am ashamed you go around Paris like that."

"No, Mr. Gasar. These shoes are made of harder leather."

Mr. Gasar would then sigh and pack up his shoes, knowing that he'd have to make several more trips to the Avenue George V before the matter was settled.

But on one occasion, I don't remember why, Mil, accompanied by Steph, made the long and tedious expedition to Mr. Gasar's flat, in the far reaches at the top of Montmartre, where his living quarters and workshop were under one roof.

The Hohenlohe ladies found his apartment impeccably clean and tidy, and while Mil, Mr. Gasar, and the painful shoes were occupied in one corner,

Steph spied a large aquarium and made a beeline for it. The aquarium was full of water as clean as Mr. Gasar's flat, and in it a lot of pretty goldfish swam about most merrily.

"What," Steph asked Mr. Gasar over her shoulder, "do you feed them?"

"Nothing, gracious lady. I never give them anything. The pet shop where I bought them four years ago said never to feed them."

Steph heard this with horror, and her kindly heart missed a beat. No food at all for all of four years! Why the poor fish! What a dreadful fate!

Another, and totally unnecessary expedition to Mr. Gasar's flat at the top of Montmartre was organized, and while Mil and Mr. Gasar and a pair of painful shoes were busy, Steph, with the dexterity of a circus magician, threw a package of fish food into the aquarium. The fish swam for it greedily, and in no time there was nothing left. The water was as clear as before, and Steph felt proudly virtuous.

The next shoe fitting took place at our apartment.

"And how are your fish, Mr. Gasar?" Steph inquired. Her question was purely rhetorical. She knew perfectly well that the fish could only be thriving.

"My fish are all dead, gracious lady. I can't understand it. My wife and I are so sad. They died soon after your second visit to our apartment."

Pope Pius XI

"He has no right, no right at all, to that second plume on his hat. Such liberties are an outrage! I shall report him to the first master of the chamber, Cardinal Caccia Dominioni."

A cavalier of the cape and sword was whispering mordacious comments in my ear about a colleague as we waited for the Pope. It seemed to me, in whose life a private audience with the Holy Father was not a daily occurrence, that he might well have desisted from caustic conversation at that particular moment. His Holiness was expected any minute. And Pius XI was always most punctual.

No sooner had the cavalier withdrawn to his post by the door than the belittled colleague approached me. His face expressed the inexpressible quite adequately.

"That man, that impossible man!" he began. "I do hope he has not bored Your Highness unduly."

Attempting not to commit myself, I thanked him for his solicitude.

To Steph, sulking alone in one corner, neither of them paid any attention. They took her at best for my governess. And no wonder! To meet the strict specifications of the Secretary of State, Cardinal Gasparri, she had ordered for the Easter audience with

Pius a smart black frock and mantilla in Milan. But, like the mantilla, the gown was of lace and through its sleeves could be seen the flesh of her arms.

"I'm afraid this won't do," said the Privy Chamberlain as soon as he saw her. "I shall send for a cloak to cover you up."

The best-dressed woman of Europe shuddered perceptibly at this suggestion and, for a few seconds, a deadly silence stormed between them. But, a short time later, a malodorous black coat was brought up from the pilgrims' checkroom and Steph was forced to slip it on. The coat was thick and heavy, apart from being far too large. It kept her at the even temperature of a slow oven on this warm Roman spring day. So she sullenly withdrew to her corner and left me a prey to the two feuding cavaliers.

There was a swish of stoles at the door. We knelt down and the Holy Father entered. He was enormously impressive in his extreme simplicity, much more so than could have been any secular ruler. Doubly noticeable against the Vatican's background of priceless splendors, his white robes and red mules were like snow with two drops of blood.

"How old are you, my son?" he asked me in fluent German, but changed his question with a gracious adroitness before I had time to answer. "I mean, of course, how young are you?"

"Twelve, Holy Father."

Then, turning affably to Steph who knelt beside me in warm discomfort, he made it quite clear by a few

*"How young are you?" asked the Pope
in German, at the Vatican.*

deft phrases and without naming any names, that in his eyes she had been greatly sinned against by my father. Their divorce had naturally never been recognized by the Church in Rome and was no more than a civil formality of the Austrian Republic. In spite of this, Father had remarried to Countess Dessewffy, née Countess Ella Bátthyány. This ceremony was contracted in the Protestant faith which had obliged Father to change his religion.

The Holy Father's words gave an insight to the fantastic thoroughness of the Vatican's world-wide system of information gathering. Pius XI had obviously been briefed by one of his papal secretaries before our audience and knew to a nicety the circumstances of my parents' marital status.

Pius XI, affable, smiling and gentle, an outdoors man and a linguist, had been an assiduous mountain climber before his election to the Holy See. He had about him an air of one who cherishes wide open spaces. It was difficult to reconcile this dignified pontiff with accusations of the cabal that, hailing from Milan, he had surrounded himself with a coterie of Milanese prelates. Even the way he presented his ring to be kissed was almost humble. To me, he was a father figure. When, at the end of our audience, I received his benediction, he empowered me to bestow it on those I loved. This gratified me immensely. I felt like a delegate Pope.

It was well after two when we returned to the Excelsior Hotel, for the Pope lunched late and the last audience of his incredibly busy morning was held around half past one. My contact with things spiritual had not robbed me of a temporal appetite. (Although I must admit that between the audience with the Pope and climbing the holy staircase a few days later on our knees, saying a prayer on each step for which all one's sins are remitted made me feel pious as hell.) As we descended in the Vatican elevator with its glass panels representing the passion of Jesus Christ, I planned on a menu of blue trout and corn on the cob, both out of season. Impressed though I was with a private audience with the Pope, I was still and all a very hungry twelve-year-old boy!

The detour via Monte Carlo

I must have been about ten years old. My parents and I were on a motor trip through Europe during my summer vacation from school. The three of us were dedicated motorists and would drive for hundreds of miles over good roads and bad, in all kinds of weather, through practically every European country.

The first car that I can remember was Steph's electric brougham for town use only. It had two elegant lanterns, one on either side of the door. The chauffeur, still called a watman, sat outside whatever the temperature.

Our next car was a red Austro-Daimler convertible with a steering wheel that lifted up as a safeguard against theft when the car was parked. This was followed in time by a very dashing Chenard & Walker torpedo, yellow with a silver bonnet. There were two windshields, one in front and one in back for the rear seat passengers. Days when we would stop to raise the top were few. We considered "indoor driving" terribly sissy. It took a great deal of rain or snow, or on one occasion my breaking out with the measles in the middle of a trip, to make us turn the car with its celluloid side windows, into a saloon.

Later still came a wonderful midnight blue Hispano-Suiza with an extra long body especially designed and built for us by Kellner of Paris, the best French coach builder of his time. No insurance company of that period would insure it because of its great length.

There were a string of Rolls-Royces with bodies by Barker Bros. of Saint James Street, London. I think eleven of these. Always we sat in front, three abreast, leaving the warmth and comfort of the back to the chauffeur, maid and dogs.

I relished these trips. Some of my happiest childhood memories are of speeding down Signor Mussolini's

*Mostyen, our chauffeur, with Steph
and Countess Pita du Boisrouvray
beside Steph's golden Rolls-Royce.*

newly invented paying autostrada between Milan and the Italian lakes, with a roaring open exhaust pipe.

On one trip we had been on the road for several weeks when our consciences began to bother us. Mil, who had elected to spend the summer in Monte Carlo, was all alone. We felt that she would be pleased if we paid her a short visit.

The Principality of Monaco was completely out of our way. I think we were in Holland at the time. But never mind—filial duty came first. She would be so very happy to see us.

The French Riviera had not yet been discovered as a summer playground. Monte Carlo in the heat of August was a sleepy little town, slightly dusty, and very charming. Not a single skyscraper had yet been built; nor had the sporting d'été, or the beach hotels. If the few summer holiday seekers wanted to swim, there was the Plage du Larvotto, with lots of pebbles and wooden cabins smelling of salt, sand and sunshine. One took a horse-drawn buggy to reach it. The trains from France and Italy puffed by between the Casino and the Mediterranean. Air conditioning was, of course, totally unknown. To insure a degree of comfort from the heat, one's rooms lay in pleasant coolness during the day behind lowered shades. At night everyone slept under vast, white mosquito nettings.

We thought we would surprise Mil, so we did not send her a telegram to announce our arrival. Our schedule was arranged so that we reached Monte Carlo in the morning to be sure to find her still at her hotel.

Calling her from downstairs, we would say "Good morning," and not let on where we were. Then, only after she would ask us where we were calling from, would we chirp "Surprise! Surprise! We are here in the lobby." That is what we thought we would do.

The scenario of what really happened turned out somewhat differently. When we asked for her room number the porter said: "Madame est sortie."

This put a small dampener on our enthusiasm. She must have gone out to do some early shopping. Where else would a reasonable old lady go at this hour in the morning?

We checked in. Rooms in those happy days were plentiful during the off season. No need for reservations.

When Mil had not returned an hour later, we asked the porter if he knew where she might have gone. "But yes. Naturellement," he said. "Madame has gone to the Casino. Madame goes to the Casino every morning."

At that time the Casino of Monte Carlo was probably the only place in the world, short of the fleshpots of Nevada and Macao, where you could gamble in the morning.

We were slightly nonplussed, and forthwith sent a messenger to that den of iniquity with the glad tidings that we had arrived. We expected this message to catapult her into our loving arms without delay. A few minutes more and she would be here, delighted that we had made such a detour just to see her.

But we hadn't reckoned with the magnetic lure of the spinning roulette wheel. Madame sent back word that she was enchanted to hear that we had arrived in Monte Carlo, but she was on a winning streak and couldn't leave the tables just now. She would see us a little later.

We waited until lunchtime. Mil had a healthy appetite, so of course she would show up for lunch. Besides, wasn't she on demipension? Would a thrifty Hausfrau like she forego a meal she had already paid for? Again we were mistaken.

Around two o'clock we sent a second bellboy to seek her. He, too returned without his quarry, and the alarming message: "Madame was now on a losing streak, and could not possibly leave the Casino before she recouped her losses."

After this, exhausted from our night's hard driving, we retired to our respective rooms, and had a well deserved siesta.

When we awakened at tea time there was still no sign of our delinquent relative, but knowing how addicted she was to her afternoon coffee, an irradicable habit of Viennese life, we felt certain that she would arrive momentarily. Time went by, and still Mil did not show up.

My parents could have gone to the Casino, but this would have meant unpacking—a certain type of clothing was deemed essential dress even during the off season in the Casino. This they did not want to do, as we only intended to stay overnight before resuming our travels in goggles and white linen dusters.

Around sixish, a third messenger was sent off to

ascertain whether Madame was still in hot pursuit of an upturn streak. The reply he brought back was Delphic. She was neither winning, nor was she losing.

That night we dined alone, as we had breakfasted, lunched, and tea'd.

Mil showed up around midnight and found us asleep. She woke us up, each one in turn, to say how happy she was that we were there, and how she had longed all day to see us.

Sports until one's tongue hangs out

In order to toughen me up for the life that lay ahead of me, and which they rightly guessed would not always be easy, both of my parents resorted to a number of devices which may have seemed unorthodox, but which worked very well. Not only was I driven relentlessly to compete in every kind of game or sport, but I was also made to travel on my own at a very early age to sharpen my skills in looking after myself. I was sent to boarding school before I knew how to spell my own name.

I was never told not to smoke or drink, although it was probably hoped that I wouldn't. If I don't do either to this day, it is undoubtedly because they were not made to seem the forbidden fruit to me. Along the same line of thinking, grown-up parties never held any secrets for me because my parents felt that knowing what life was all about could only teach me to avoid its pitfalls. The tea dances of the Riviera and the ski slopes of Gstaad were all one. All good to teach me something and knock any latent nonsense out of me.

Rightly—or wrongly—it was considered early on in my life that I had an aptitude for games far greater than my talents for academic pursuits. Consequently, beginning with my immersion into the Adriatic Sea before I could walk, closely followed by a dunking in the deep end of a swimming pool in Baden bei Wien, to see if I would drown or float, I was pushed, badgered, encouraged, driven, trained and promoted by a madly competitive family into every conceivable form of outdoor exercise.

In the course of time I was made to row, sail, paddle, fence, surf, ride, drive, water-ski, box, skate, ski, toboggan, curl, bowl, skin dive, cycle, shoot, fish, run, jump, long jump, pole vault, play golf, tennis, football, volley ball, squash, ping-pong, and basketball.

Since it is totally impossible to be a natural born athlete in so many different kinds of sports, I was

Every sport imaginable.

driven by my relentless parents and grandparents until they had succeeded in shaming me in such a way that I won a few skiing medals, one or two prizes in junior gymkhanas, a place on the swimming team of my school, another on the fencing team. I also rowed for my college at the Marlowe regattas, held a blue at Oxford for swimming on the varsity team, and finally made the Olympic tryouts. Not a formidably impressive career, but it kept the family moderately happy. Pop never missed an occasion to show me off by bidding me to jump into any body of water, at any temperature, to do the butterfly stroke.

But Grandmother Mil was the keenest of my tyrant coaches. She would come and see me swim in as many meets as she could attend. Not as might be expected in a mood of grandmotherly benevolence, but with a sharp and critical eye. At the end of the meets, and before the other team and ours went off to celebrate, she would wait for me outside the baths or stadium, sitting in her limousine with our chauffeur standing by. There in the back seat of the car I would get the critique of my day's performance.

"Your start was slow, though better than at your meet against Bournemouth. Your turns were bad. You could gain another three seconds at least in the hundred yards. Why did you let that Rhodes scholar yokel push you out of your lane? We shall have to work on all that this summer in Monte Carlo."

Oh, those summers in Monte Carlo, after the Beach Club had been built! There I was, while other youngsters were happily splashing about or playing volleyball by the side of the Olympic pool, starting and turning. Mil in her straw hat would stand by, stop watch in hand, making me repeat my weakest points over and over and over again.

But apparently all this insistence on excellence in sports did not leave too shattering a mark on my psyche. For on top of everything I was coerced into doing, I had a secret yearning to pilot a plane. My family for some inexplicable reason was dead set against it. As a consequence, I had to take my flying lessons behind their backs using my own money. Something must have been lacking. Perhaps the family encouragement I'd always had before. I turned out to be a very mediocre pilot, and gave up before ever getting my license.

The Aga Khan

The Aga Khan—all 280 pounds of him—and my family had in common a predilection for Deauville in the summer, and the Ritz on "servant vacation time." My meetings with him often took place in one or the other of these two glamour spots: Deauville where he owned a villa or the Ritz where he maintained a suite of rooms, and where I could frequently be found re-running the chariot races of Ben Hur in the long corridors. I was the heroic charioteer; while the horses' roles were played to perfection by two long-suffering, but willing Skye terriers. The chariot itself was often constructed out of one of Steph's hat boxes.

On some occasions, especially if it was siesta time, the Aga, looking like a benevolent owl behind his thick-lensed glasses, would interrupt these antic games in the interest of peace and quiet. Then, beckoning me to come to his suite, he would ply me with boxes of Turkish Delight of which both he and I were inordinately fond. Since nobody else ever thought of giving me more than one piece of this gooey delicacy at a time, the generous Aga ranked high in my esteem. No doubt he felt that my sporting instincts boded well, for was he himself not the owner of a famous racing stable? Of course, his gifts had to be carried back to our quarters in stealth and disposed of behind locked doors as discovery would have meant confiscation.

Years later, long after this benefactor's demise, I was having lunch one day with his younger son, Prince Sadruddin Khan, in Geneva. I told him the story of his father's frequent gifts of Turkish Delight. "But where," I asked Sadri, "do you suppose he got such an endless supply of the stuff?"

Sadri Khan, who has a deadpan sense of humor, beckoned me to come closer; obviously to confer on me

a well kept secret. As I leaned forward waiting for a revelation, he whispered: "We owned a small sweet shop in Plan-les-Ovates" (a suburb of Geneva). "Father worked late at night rolling dough. That's how he made all his money."

Ironically Sadri's mother, the Aga's last but one wife, did work in a small sweet shop in Aix-les-Baine when the Aga first met her.

The Aga Khan at his villa with his wife before last, Princess Andrée, mother of Prince Sadruddin Khan.

71

Signor Perugia

I sometimes accompanied Steph on her almost daily rounds which took her from Van Cleef & Arpels or Chaumet or Cartier, her jewelers, to Chanel or Paquin, her dressmakers, to Caroline Reboux, her hat maker. But far above all these important errands came Perugia who made her shoes.

There were few boot makers in Paris that women of fashion patronized: Greco, Hellstern, and Lobb. But the latter only for riding boots. Floating above all of these, on a cloud all his own, was Perugia, the marvel from Italy, who made the finest shoes of them all. Steph was addicted to Perugia, and Perugia was addicted to her— as well he might be, for we all felt that she had already spent enough in his store to ensure a golden retirement for him, his wife, and all their children.

On this particular day Steph entered Perugia's store on the rue de la Paix. I followed behind with two Skye terriers on a double leash, and no doubt weighted down by sundry pieces of wearing apparel that had to be returned for readjustments. Oh Lord! The patience those sales ladies had in those days! Mr. Perugia greeted Steph affably as was his custom, but the words that came out of his mouth were these:

"Madame la Princesse," he said, "you are one of my best, nay, my best customer. Dozens of ladies have come to my shop because they saw shoes on your feet which I have made for you. Your taste is impeccable. You set the styles. You are one of the most elegant women in Paris. But I beseech you when you leave this store today never come again. You are driving me and all the employees in my workshop crazy. I tremble when I see you open your handbag and pull out your tape measure to tell me that your green dancing slippers are a quarter of an inch too high or too low. The blue satin evening shoes we dyed for you last month went back six times because the shade was never quite right. I have had to redo your last golf shoes seven times! My nerves won't stand any more. Please go and never come back."

I stood there thunderstruck, not believing my ears. Steph stood there too. But she, at least, did not look thunderstruck at all. She put her tape measure, which Mr. Perugia feared so much, back in her Cartier handbag and snapped the tortoise-shell clasp shut. Then she turned on her heels (possibly one-eighth of an inch too low?) and left the shop. I, still thunderstruck, followed her. But outside, on the pavement, I gave vent to my astonishment.

"I can't believe it," I said. "You let Perugia throw you out of his store and never batted an eyelash! And who will now make your shoes for you?"

"Perugia."

"But he just told you never to come back!"

"Nonsense. Perugia needs me. I am his inspiration and he knows it. He is a superb craftsman, but he has no imagination at all. I feed him ideas. Without me and a handful of other women in Paris, he might as well close shop. There is Madame Muñoz, Ia Abdy, Dulcie Martinez de Hoz, Charlie Brighton, and me. We are the locomotives of Paris and he needs us."

I knew all these women, except Charlie Brighton, who was a cocotte. But I knew all about her. She was the quintessence of chic—not at all what you'd expect from a lady who made her living horizontally with very rich gentlemen. She owned a beige and black coupé de ville Rolls-Royce, and her chauffeur and footman, who sat in front, were dressed in beige and black to match the colors of the car. Charlie's hair was cut very short in a fashionable Eton crop, and she looked like a mischievous schoolboy.

A week later Steph entered Perugia's again, laden with color samples, and with the tape measure, I'm sure, stuck away in her handbag.

Perugia greeted her with obvious relief, and no one ever again spoke of the throwing-out incident. He was all too happy to have her back, for she was really, as both of them well knew, his inspiration.

Joan of Arc

It was the birthday of Joan of Arc. I don't remember which one. Perhaps the 500th. Or was it the day on which she had been burned at the stake that was being celebrated? Hardly, I'd say—France being a Catholic country. Whichever it was, celebrations were being prepared all over France, especially in Rouen where the poor young woman had come to such a bad end. Since I was in school in Normandy, sixteen kilometers from Rouen, we felt the vibrations very strongly. The city council—no doubt to compensate for its shameful behavior five centuries before—was preparing celebrations on an unheard of scale. There were going to be illuminations of course, a solemn mass or two, as goes without saying, speeches naturally, and even a display of units of the French fleet, unexpectedly, in the deep river harbor of the Seine. Cider, the local drink, would be distributed free of charge to the thirsty.

In my class one of my closest buddies was Jacquie Vilgrain. I liked him very much, although he was the only one in school who could (almost) beat me in the hundred meters breast stroke. He could also, like I, cross the lake of Fuschl, breast stroke or crawl, when he came and stayed with us in Austria during summer vacations. Jacquie, in other words, was a fine lad. But he had a screw loose where ships were concerned.

Nothing excited him as much as the sight of a destroyer, an airplane carrier, or a submarine. He knew as much about "Jane's Fighting Ships" as the man who wrote it. When the newspapers announced that a submarine would be among the ships on display in Rouen during the celebration, and that this sub would be open to visitors, there was no holding him back. Jacquie decided that such an opportunity could not be missed. He had to, simply had to, get himself to Rouen (which was totally out of bounds to us, of course). And since this could not be done openly, in daytime, he would get to Rouen somehow at night.

Jacquie came from a very prosperous family. The Vilgrains, owners of the "Moulins de Paris," had provided most of France with flour for almost three hundred years. Yet being the scion of a rich family in France does not mean that you get a rich allowance. Far from it. Jacquie's pocket money was no more than that of any of us. He had, by this time, concocted a scenario in his head which involved getting to Rouen at night by taxi. And for such an enterprise he needed co-financiers. He rode on his bicycle to a far off village one afternoon and found a taxi—the only taxi in that rural community. The owner-driver of this ancient vehicle was no fool and knew exactly that what Jacquie was hiring him for was illegal. But as this taxi was never used in this small village except for funerals, and then only for the older people for whom the walk to the cemetery was too arduous, he saw his chance to make a little unexpected money and consented.

Jacquie had by this time whipped four of us into a state of enthusiasm, with me his buddy-buddy included. The taxi was to meet us at half-past nine o'clock by a corner between the piano teacher's house and the vegetable garden. We, the four conspirators, were to leave by a window we knew to be easy to open above one of the johns next to the football lockers in the basement. This window, giving on the back of the house, was as far as we could get from the housemaster's private quarters. Before leaving, each of us stuffed sweat shirts, swim trunks and dirty socks into our beds, to look as much like us as possible. One never knew. The housemaster had good ears and might come snooping around with a torchlight. Fortunately he didn't, for the "bodies" we left behind in our beds looked very much like scarecrows and very little like boys.

But nothing untoward happened. The taxi was there to meet us at the appointed time and place, and we sighed with relief when we realized our fugue had gone undetected. Soon we were in Rouen, and leaving our taxi with instructions to pick us up again at midnight, we started the rounds of sight-seeing. Naturally Jacquie's ships came first, for it was because of them that the whole thing had been engineered!

The quais of the Seine were brightly illuminated, as were all the spots of interest in the entire city. We went from one sight to another, and when everything of note had been taken in, our thoughts turned elsewhere. They turned to a street, a certain street, of which all of us at school had heard, but where none of us had ever been. The street of red lanterns! At first we had trouble finding it because none of us dared come right out and ask a passerby for its location. Finally we found it, and were, if the truth be told, quite disappointed with its size. It was a short street in an old part of Rouen, with not too many lanterns hanging in front of not too many small houses. Even so, we wanted to see what happened behind those doors.

We had hardly entered the first of these brothels when we were speedily expelled. We tried several other red light houses with the same sad result, and I have to confess that the reason for these fast rejections was principally me. I still had a very round and babyish face at pre-fourteen; my nickname at school was in fact, "Bébé." It was contemplated for awhile that I might be left standing outside while the others, more mature looking than I, would be given the chance of attending to more serious matters inside. But in the end this scheme was judged too cruel to me and was abandoned. Midnight saw us at the appointed place where our taxi and driver were waiting, and we drove back to school.

For me this one and only time was the end of the nocturnal adventures, but the others went again several times. The rumors of their derring-do soon spread from classroom to classroom, until it reached the ears of Louis Dedet, our ex-international rugger player headmaster. There followed a big scandal and some expulsions. Inevitably the clamor arose, "And what about Bébé?"

The headmaster, whose great favorite I was, and

who had my photograph in football gear standing on his desk, turned a deaf ear to this gossip. Besides, he hated snitchers. I was never sent down, not even summoned to his study. My baby face had saved me.

The very first time

When I was past fourteen but not yet fifteen, and totally virginal, some of the "big boys" at school, the Collège de Normandie, decreed that such a shameful state could not be endured much longer. I would have to be initiated into the sex rites of my peers and elders (who were no more than sixteen). The time for my initiation would be during Christmas vacation, which most of us spent in Paris in the heart of our loving families. All the loving families, even if they were Indian, Brazilian, Mexican, or Norwegian, owned houses or apartments in the French capital.

My guide and mentor who offered to show me the "right way" was Pierre Tawil. He was French but his family had made its fortune in Egypt. When in Paris they lived at the Lutetia Hotel, which gave him a lot of freedom of action. He was a rake and had much experience with young "ladies." One of his front teeth was chipped, and he wore his dark hair plastered down with gomina argentina, as was the fashion. None of this made him look any better, but nonetheless he had great success with the female sex.

Mr. Tawil Sr. and his wife drove down from Paris every Sunday, in a very sporty Hispano-Suiza, to visit their son, which made us all green with envy. My family came once a term, rather reluctantly, and the rest of the time, when they thought of it, they dispatched Ernst.

Pierre came to fetch me at our apartment one cold and rainy December afternoon, for although he was, I was not allowed to go out alone. We took a taxi and drove to the Boulevard des Italiens where Pierre had arranged to meet one of his many "ladies" at a certain café. He promised me that she was very pretty, and she would act as my initiator. She was already there when we arrived at the café, and it was true—she was pretty. Of course she was also a very old woman, 23 years of age, but blonde, and Polish, and friendly, and cheerful. I liked her.

We set out in another taxi—not because we were going very far, but on account of the weather—and drove to a rather sad looking small hotel next to the Folies Bergère. There, a friend of the blonde Pole was to while away Pierre's time during my initiation. The friend was there: small, skinny, mousy-haired, and fussy. I hated her on sight, and all the desire that had been building up in me quickly subsided. Pierre quite obviously saw her as I did, for he quickly decided in a complete about-turn that the blonde Pole would after all be better suited for him, since they knew each other so well, while I could learn just as easily with the little mouse.

We repaired, he and I, to two different rooms—each with his "lady." I was rather stunned by Pierre's fast thinking and speedy military maneuver which left me stranded with this chatterbox and her frizzy, mousy hair.

She proceeded to undress, and I, in order to untie the laces of my shoes, sat down on the bed. This brought out a loud screech from her. Without realizing it I had sat on a deplorable rabbit fur coat which she decreed was most precious. I apologized and placed my behind on the bedspread instead.

Finally all the preparations had been accomplished and the frizzy-haired mouse proceeded to a washbasin hidden behind a screen and came back with a wet washcloth that seemed gray and dubious to me. With this instrument, in a few experienced, rough gestures, she proceeded to scrub the most intimate part of my anatomy, thereby causing it great pain. I let out a loud

At the Collège de Normandie.

yell and she dropped her insalubrious washcloth.

"Oh dear! Oh dear!" she screamed. "You are infected. And now I shall have caught it from you. Always I have been so careful, so clean, so meticulous. And now you've given me that terrible disease!"

Exactly what terrible disease she thought I had given her was unclear in my mind, since there are several from which to choose. Since nothing other than the vigorous washcloth had passed between us, it was difficult to see how I could have infected her. But she went on lamenting herself, and opening wide the door of our room which led into the passage, ran out, stark naked save for stockings, garters, and high-heeled shoes.

Her racket caused one door after another to open in turn. People in various stages of undress came out to see what all the noise was about. Men in underwear and without began pouring into my room where I sat like Buddha, devoid of clothes, in the middle of the bed where the ministrations of the mouse had left me. The only one totally dressed, the maid, came in as well, and there was much shaking of heads at the thought that someone so young could already be so depraved.

The noise and confusion had also disturbed Pierre Tawil, in his room a few doors down. He too came out to see what was happening. When he found out, he spoke these noble words for all to hear and for which I was of course immensely grateful to him:

"Stupid hysterical cow!" he exclaimed. "Stop all that noise you are making. He is fourteen and has never yet screwed."

The Duke of Westminster

The Duke of Westminster was probably the richest man in England. All that part of London known as the City of Westminster belonged to him, not forgetting Westminster Abbey and Westminster Cathedral; also a goodly chunk of Mayfair. He was also an eccentric. This eccentricity had begun at birth when his parents christened him Bendor after a horse.

He'd had a liaison with Coco Chanel. But by the time my story starts this had cooled off considerably, and people said that the cooling off had been done by Coco Chanel herself.

He then turned his attention to Steph, who, all independent woman though she was, must have turned weak in the knees at the thought of all those millions. Bendor had several wives in his past by then, and several ahead of him, which did not prevent him from asking Steph up to Scotland for some fishing.

No doubt Steph the all-around sportswoman, who shamed men tall and stalwart when out chamois hunting, or skiing, or sailing, saw herself casting a mean fly in those Scottish waters, to the astonishment and admiration of the eccentric Duke.

She packed her warmest cashmeres and her tweediest tweeds, and her best Lobb walking and stalking shoes, and off to Scotland she went. There on arrival, alas, a slight contretemps awaited her. Lady Ursula Filmer-Sanky, Bendor's very much grown-up daughter by one of the former wives, was also present. Now, as every woman knows, a daughter by a former marriage can only look askance at any new female in the vicinity of her dear papa. Lady Ursula was no exception. The conversation at the first dinner on the first evening was cool; let us say like the salmon waters of Scotland. But never mind—Steph was determined to wrest admirative expletives from her Duke the following morning when he saw her in hip boots, immersed up to here in an icy stream.

The next morning came. Dawn had not yet broken, and there was a knock on her door. It was her gillie, the one dispatched to accompany her all day while fishing. They made for a dark and forbidding loch, the gillie and she, no one else.

"Where is His Grace?" Steph wanted to know, not unnaturally.

"Ach," said the gillie, or some other such Scottish expression. "His Grace is fishing on another loch."

"Well, well," said Steph, as she took this in. But she continued standing in the icy water in her rubber hip boots. And that night, over haggis and kedgeree, she inquired if Bendor would continue to fish a different loch from hers.

"That I will," he said. "Women fishing make me nervous. One never knows where they'll cast their flies."

Meanwhile the conversation, with Lady Ursula still

at the table, was no more cozy than the night before.

Steph stood this another three days, after which she packed her lovely tweeds, her lovely cashmeres, her sturdy boots, and headed back to town. Let Mademoiselle Chanel have Bendor if she still wanted him.

As a postscript I should like to add this anecdote. One of his wives, unable to stand it a minute longer, threw a mink coat over her chiffon nightshirt and ran for the station, albeit not too fast as she was wearing bedroom slippers. There in the middle of the night she boarded a train for Paris and initiated divorce proceedings. The authenticity of this tale was guaranteed to me between algebra and Latin lessons, by her son from another marriage, with whom I sat on the school bench.

Margot Oxford

The Countess of Oxford and Asquith, born Margot Tennant, and widow of a former British Prime Minister, was a highly original lady, known in all of London, and feared by many. Her tongue was as sharp as her profile. But in spite or perhaps because of this she was one of Steph's intimate friends. She was an eagerly awaited guest when she came and stayed with us during our summers in Fuschl.

Since she kept a large house in London where she did a great deal of entertaining, and was always spending more than she should have, kind-hearted Steph had induced Lord Rothermere to let Margot write a column for the *Daily Mail.* She liked that job. It gave her much freedom, and had a large readership of fans (as well as enemies).

Whenever she came to Fuschl she was accompanied by her secretary, Miss Campbell, whom everyone adored, and a lady's maid lent to her for the summer by her daughter, Princess Bibesco. Margot's daughter, Elizabeth, had married a Romanian diplomat, Prince Antoine Bibesco, and always dispensed with her maid's services during the summer months.

Lady Oxford was of the opinion that people sleep far too many hours every night. She claimed that she needed only four hours of sleep, and as a result was wide awake while ordinary human beings were still in the arms of Morpheus. She used these early hours to write her column. Comfortably settled in her bed, and with a bottle of brandy by her side, she would put to paper her thoughts on all manner of subjects.

Each evening as she turned down the bed, Princess Bibesco's maid, who knew Lady Oxford's habits, would set a fresh bottle of brandy (out of Steph's reserves) on the night table by her bedside. The bottles, usually well on their way to emptiness the following morning, gave Margot her inspiration. She made her first appearance of the day around lunchtime, in top form, and never ever showing any signs of having hit the bottle too heavily. Margot was quite a woman.

Long before this tardy appearance for lunch, I, who am also an early riser, would receive notes from Margot, brought by one of the footmen from the main house where her room was located, to the annex where I had my own room together with all the junior crowd among the guests. The notes might read as follows:

"Darling Boy—

Your mother is such a silly goose. She always lets herself be swamped by all these uninvited guests! She can never say an energetic no. Who is this Countess Mercati who dropped in so unexpectedly in her huge Cadillac yesterday? And who were all those ghastly people with the Vicomtesse de Noailles? How ugly that dreadful woman is! Quite revolting. Young Jimmy Donohue is a lout. I'm sure we shall again be at least

*Steph, Archduke Franz Salvator
and Lady Oxford.*

twenty for lunch. It's because of that I can never have a quiet game of golf with Steph and Mostyn. What is the name of the Italian national anthem? I was received in the Spring by that clown Mussolini in Rome. He showed up in riding boots! I asked him if he had just stepped off a horse. I can see your tutor Eric Overell through my window. He seems to be inspecting the tennis court to see if it's dry enough to play on. What are we having for lunch? —Margot.

A game of bridge

In our house in Fuschl, during the summer, there were many games of bridge, always in the afternoon, but mostly when it was raining, which in the Salzkammergut means very often. On this particular afternoon, however, the weather was especially warm and sunny— yet in spite of that a game of bridge had been organized after lunch, out in the garden. Two gentlemen and two ladies were sitting around the table: the Archduke Franz

Steph and Professor Fritz Kreisler.

Salvator, the Maharaja of Kapurthala, Lady Oxford and Asquith, and Steph, by far the least talented player of the four.

Baron Maurice de Rothschild (the very same one Anna had thrown out manu militari from Steph's suite at the Royal Hotel in Deauville a few seasons ago) had felt the urge, seeing how sultry the weather was, of taking a little nap after lunch, and had been shown to a horsehair chaise longue which stood on the first floor landing. He had fallen asleep immediately, as was attested by his loud snoring.

Countess Amaury du Boisrouvrasy, our beloved Pita, Rainier de Monaco's aunt, who also spent every summer with us in Austria, had meanwhile decided to give her formerly lovely voice some exercise. She had inveigled Fritz Kreisler, the famous violinist and composer of such operettas as "Sissi," to accompany her on the piano. They had retired to the living room and Pita's voice could be heard through the windows, in operatic arias. Unfortunately, Pita's voice and Maurice de Rothschild's snores were less than well synchronized. The combined racket was awful.

After a while Margot Oxford had enough of it. She could no longer concentrate on the cards and got up from the table. Standing there facing the house, she shouted, "Shut your bloody mouths, the two of you! I don't know which one of you sounds worse!"

Pita, offended, stopped right away. Maurice, whom nothing could offend, went right on snoring.

Modern art

I passed my baccalaureate at the Sorbonne in Paris at sixteen, and with this bachelier ès lettres secure in my pocket, was straightaway sent to Oxford where my name was entered at Magdalen College almost since birth.

My years there, which count as some of the happiest of my life, pigeonholed me as a bruiser. Already in France, at the Collège de Normandie, where I had learned my three R's, I had boxed, swum, ridden, fenced, canoed, thrown the javelin, cycled, run cross-countries, played tennis, football, volleyball, basketball, and luged on the rare winters when the Norman weather provided the snow for it.

Now, at Oxford, I added golf and rowing, while continuing to swim, ride, box and fence. Since I swam on the Oxford varsity team and rowed in one of my college eights, this left little time for academic studies. The B.A. and M.A. which I did finally get, were obtained by the skin of my teeth.

Not surprisingly, all my friends saw me as the prototype of the hearty non-intellectual. Although this did not disturb me very much, it did occur to me that it would be fun one day to surprise them! What could I do to surprise them, short of becoming a great scholar overnight, which seemed hardly likely? I gave this considerable thought and came up with several solutions. First of all, since I at least knew how to spell cat, and a few subsidiary words as well, why not write for one of the local papers? Sure enough, after no time at all, I got an assignment from the undergraduate *Isis* to contribute a weekly column. A little later I was made the same offer by the rival *Cherwell*. I accepted them both.

So much for literature. But a picture exhibition would be even nicer, although I did not know how to paint and had no pictures to exhibit. That bridge I decided to cross when I got to it. I must confess, though, that I had always known how to draw after a fashion and had even shown a certain naïve-sophisticated promise. But that was all. It went no further than that.

When this idea of an exhibition had jelled in my mind, I went to work. My first step was to collect a few of my old copy-books from the Collège de Normandie where, mostly in the margins of my physics and trigonometry problems, could be found pencil sketches of girls, racing cars, aeroplanes, and more girls. With these tucked under my arm, during my next trip to London, I marched to the Slade School of Art where I had a friend. This friend was Professor Polunin, distinguished teacher, artist, creator of ballet decor and costumes, whose sons Oleg and Nicolas were with me at Oxford—Oleg an undergraduate, Nicolas a young don.

I showed Professor Polunin my handiwork and asked him if he thought that with a little time and effort I might parlay these drawings into a one man show. He looked at my sketches, then at me. After that he tapped his forehead with the index of his right hand and burst out laughing. He might have been a friend but he was no liar.

Strange to relate, this did not discourage me. It merely proved, I argued to myself, that I had knocked on the wrong door. The world of Art with a capital A, as embodied by Professor Polunin and the Slade School, was not for me. My art, written small, was intended for the masses, the field of commercialism. Consequently, on my next foray to the city I would use a little showmanship. The sketches had to be framed! And off I went in search of a suitable framemaker. In time I found one. My choice could not have been more felicitous. He came from a long line of framemakers, all quite obviously superb craftsmen. He was also, thank God, totally devoid of imagination, and nothing I asked him to make surprised him in the slightest. Anyone else would have blanched and refused point blank when faced with the bizarre little numbers I asked him to construct for me. One frame was triangular, another made of thumb tacks, a third one of starched organza, and one all of glass with no wood at all. He was also hideously expensive. But with a comfortable $30,000 a year pocket money, paid into my account at the Messrs. Coutts & Co. from the Girard Trust in Philadelphia, where most of the family's nest egg was stashed away, this did not fluster me.

I started out by having no more than three of my drawings framed, and then marched off, carefully leaving them behind, to New Bond Street, mecca of some of London's more commercial picture galleries. I cased all of these from the outside and picked the largest and most prosperous looking one as a starter. It was the Fine Art Society, plush and solid.

Once inside, I asked if I might speak to the manager and handed the attendant my card. Mr. Dawbarn received me with civility and asked what he could do for me. I explained that I was an undergraduate at Oxford, not a starving young artist. In fact, I frankly admitted, I did not even wish to make a career in painting. But, for reasons too uninteresting to relate to him, I should like to have a picture exhibition—just once!

Mr. Dawbarn did not seem to think this strange or quixotic and I pushed my advantage.

"If, after you have seen my pictures," I said, "you consider them good enough to be shown publicly, I can guarantee you one thing: it will bring you masses of people who ordinarily would never dream of setting foot in a picture gallery."

He seemed to find this a pleasant idea, and I continued: "I know half of London and all of Oxford. My friends and the friends of my family will be surprised out of their wits when they hear that I'm having a picture exhibition, and they are sure to pour in here one and all—if only to see me make a fool of myself. But for whatever reason, they'll be here, and that will mean a whole football stadium of potential new customers for you."

"What pictures have you got? And when can I see them?"

"Could I ask you to come and view them at our house?" I realized that psychologically, and from every other point of view, it was preferable to show them to him under my own roof rather than lugging them under my arm to his gallery.

"All right."

"Then why don't you come for tea, say on the day after tomorrow around five?"

When he rang our doorbell, our butler Pratt, who was better than Jeeves, opened the door. Right away this made a favorable first impression on a man who knew full well the commercial value of snobbery. I gave him a jolly good tea and then proceeded to show him my six pictures. They were by then most beautifully if extravagantly framed. Added to which I had taken care to lean them against chairs and tables whose colors and lights would display them to their best advantage.

Mr. Dawbarn was amused, impressed, and quite frank, all at the same time.

"I can see, of course, that you have never had a single formal art lesson in your life," he said. He was wrong there. I'd had art class at school. It was one of the prescribed subjects of our curriculum.

"But," he went on, "that does not matter. In fact, it might have spoiled your uninhibited style. You have imagination and courage" (I'll say I had!) "and that is far more important. I'm game. Come to my office tomorrow and we shall discuss the details.

Before he departed he threw me a stumper: "By the way, how many pictures do you have?"

I had no more than the three I had shown him.

"How many do you need?" I parried.

"Oh, around forty will do. I intend to let you have the first floor. Forty pictures should be enough."

"You shall have them."

We were then in March and my one-man-show was set for May, the beginning of the London Season. Jubilant at so easy a victory, at least in its first stages, I rolled up my sleeves and went to work mass-producing thirty-seven more pictures. But as May drew nearer and the hanging day approached, I still did not quite have my full quota. Growing a little uneasy, I once again fell back on my old schoolbooks, where I had studiously doodled in the margins instead of listening to our chemistry teacher. One of these pencil sketches showed the head of a woman, and she was weeping—for no good reason; I might as easily have drawn her smiling. The paper was of the standard, cheap, school supply variety, cross-ruled. It would never do for the Fine Art Society. To hide this shortcoming I asked my paragon framemaker to stretch thin wires across all the lines, both vertical and horizontal. He did so, under the glass, and the effect was stunning! The woman now looked as though she were behind prison bars, which gave her tears a meaning. It was stupendous!

On the day of the opening a crowd of people was standing in front of that particular picture. Although it was no larger than an outsize postage stamp, I had it encased in a splendid slate-gray frame at least two feet wide and six inches deep. It was made out of several layers of molding and looked exactly like steep steps leading to the prison interior.

In the center of this large group of spectators stood a distinguished white-haired lady explaining something with many gestures to all the others. I felt that if I approached she would change the subject. But I was curious to know what she was saying. I therefore dispatched my girl Friday, June Sawrey Cookson, sister of a fellow undergraduate, to listen to the discourse of the silver-haired lady. June, who had helped me with the preparation of the show and knew exactly how it had all developed, came back shaking with laughter. The lady happened to be a friend of her family and wrote very well thought of psychological novels under the pen name of Phyllis Bottome.

FROM

MAY

4th

THE FINE ART SOCIETY
148 NEW BOND STREET, W. I
REQUEST THE PLEASURE OF THE COMPANY OF

on WEDNESDAY, MAY 4th, 1938
AT THE PRIVATE VIEW OF
" TOMORROW "
BY
PRINCE FRANZ JOSEPH HOHENLOHE WALDENBURG
THE EXHIBITION WILL BE OPENED AT THREE P.M.
BY
M. DE MAROSY, HUNGARIAN CHARGÉ D'AFFAIRES

TO

MAY

21st

The Invitation.

What she was telling her audience was this:

"You see those prison bars? It shows that the boy has pent-up emotions which need to be released but cannot come to the surface. The prison is a symbol of his inability to express himself freely. The tears are an inner sadness. The bars are a repression."

My lightly made promise to Mr. Dawbarn had been kept. The show was a roaring success for all the reasons I had anticipated. It had been opened officially by the Hungarian Chargé d'Affaires, following a luncheon given in my honor by Lady Oxford at her house on Bedford Square. All my friends and those of my parents as well, bless their little hearts, cooperated in this outrageous deception. The press had been invited and turned up with flashbulbs and cameras in unbelievable numbers. All the better debs of the season were there, and by the end of the first afternoon exactly half the pictures were sold.

In order to encourage sales right from the start, I had selected a number of my more miserable works, the ones I judged no one in his right mind would ever buy, and had generously "donated" them to a chosen number of "collectors." Mil, my mischievous grand-mother, was one of these. It enabled me to stick a red star on the picture "donated" to her, with the notation "On loan from the collection of Baroness Kálman Szepessy." Another read "By kind permission of H. Pratt Esq." Dear Pratt had a good laugh over this in the servants' hall the following morning.

It must be mentioned here that the pricing of the

pictures had given rise to a little perplexity. One day, close to the vernissage, Mr. Dawbarn had called me in to decide on the hanging of the pictures. Everything was proceeding beautifully and once in a while I had to pinch myself to see if I weren't dreaming it all, when Mr. Dawbarn turned to me and said, "Would you hand me the list of your prices?"

"My p-p-prices?" I stuttered. It had not, until that moment, ever occurred to me that he actually intended to sell my paintings. Who would be fool enough to buy them? I mumbled something unintelligible in reply, and Mr. Dawbarn, seeing that he was obviously dealing with a village idiot, took matters into his own hands. His secretary was following us, pencil and pad at the ready, as we walked along the gallery where all the pictures were now leaning against the walls.

"Forty guineas," he began dictating. "Seventy. Thirty-two. A hundred ten."

I couldn't believe my ears and suspected him of joking.

"After all," he explained to me when he had finished, "we at the Fine Art Society are paying for all the advertising. We also pay for the lights and the attendants and the printing of the programs and the buffet and the drinks." (There was a fine buffet and champagne on opening day.) "Where do you think our profit would come from if we don't even try to sell the pictures?"

Outside, on New Bond Street, a huge banner was waving in the breeze with the name of my show:

Tomorrow—an art exhibition by Prince Franz Hohenlohe.

James Laver of the Victoria and Albert Museum, curator, art historian and author, had seen the humor of it all and written a wonderful foreword in the program.

My family, meanwhile, quite mortified by all this commotion, was slowly but surely dying of embarrassment. Every mention of my name in the papers made them wince. Pop (though he had done exactly the same thing during the cubist era, when he was young) said that nothing would induce him to come to London during this time. But the greatest miracle remained intact: my pictures sold and went on selling. By the end of the show there was only one picture left, and I sold that one a year later.

The commission which the Fine Art Society took was quite modest, so that, in spite of the prohibitive cost of the frames, I still made a tidy profit.

Those outrageous frames were cause for many good-natured jibes in the press, as well they might be. One picture, called "The Women" after Clare Booth Luce's famous play, was appropriately framed in "cat skin." Actually it was ocelot and I had cut it from an old coat collar of Mil's. It sold within twenty-four hours.

Abraham Lincoln was right. You can fool some of the people all of the time and all of the people some of the time.

The Duchess of Oporto

The Duchess of Oporto was, quite frankly, an old bag. But an old bag in flapper's clothing. Mutton dressed as lamb. She was also a friend of Mil's who felt terribly sorry for her because the Duchess had no home. She was forced when in Paris to live at the Ritz, and when in New York at the Ritz Carlton. No sadder fate could befall a woman, Mil felt. So what with one thing and another, and her being homeless, one had to be kind to her. She was an American and her husband, long since deceased, had been a member of the royal House of Portugal. The duchess of Oporto's skirts rarely met her knees, and on her face was a deployment of all the colors of the rainbow.

Chancing upon her one day in the long passage that links together the two parts of the Ritz Hotel in Paris, Mil, wishing to be amiable, said "How young you look today." The "today" was de trop.

"But I am young," retorted the Duchess, who was then in her seventies. Mil was not. She was younger.

It chanced that at the tail end of my first solo trip to America, when I was sixteen, the Duchess, poor homeless woman, was in residence at the Ritz Carlton in New York.

"Don't you dare," Mil had written in her last letter to me, "come back to Europe without having invited that poor Duchess at least once. Remember, she is homeless!"

Next morning, after receiving this injunction, I rang up the skinny old bag—I mean the Duchess—and invited her to lunch. She was delighted to accept, she said, but would I mind taking her to dinner instead? I had forgotten her reluctance to face too much daylight. So dinner it was. I took her to El Morocco, then the number one supper club in the Big Apple, for though I was sixteen and this was my first time in the U.S.A., I knew what was what.

I picked her up at the Ritz. We drove to El Morocco and had dinner—a delicious dinner, I may add. As I was paying the bill, I made what I regarded as a polite inquiry.

"Would you perhaps like to go somewhere else?"

Surely, I thought, no respectable dowager of her years would be likely to want to go gallivanting about the streets of New York at this hour with a sixteen year old boy! But I was sorely mistaken.

"Why, what a lovely idea," she replied.

Of course, though I had known about El Morocco, that was also just about all. Other fleshpots I had not heard of. So I sought counsel from the head waiter, and he in turn inquired from John Perona—the owner of El Morocco, himself.

"Though I have not been there," said Perona, "I have heard people speak favorably of a new nightclub in Harlem," and he named it. So I and the duchess got into another taxi and drove those miles and miles up

north, until we were in the heart of New York's "colored
district." We were deposited at the night spot Perona
had recommended. The floor show had already begun,
but while the waiter showed us to a table and we
settled down, ordered, and took our bearings, neither of
us paid much attention to it. When we finally did, and
took in what was happening on that floor, my eyes
popped out of their sockets. Never in all my life would
I have thought it possible to see such bedroom
movements displayed in public! I did not dare to look
at my guest, and she, quite obviously, was trying hard
to refrain from looking at me. Our embarrassment could
be cut with a knife, and I saw her back to her hotel as
soon as the pornographic show had ended.

I had certainly done more than my duty by Mil's
old friend, the homeless Duchess.

Prince Chichibu

While an undergraduate at Oxford I played golf, rode horseback, boxed, fenced, swam on the Oxford University swimming team, and rowed for Magdalen, my college. I also studied a little. Not much.

Eights week (Oxford's regatta) takes place during the last term of the scholastic year. It is a very colorful, festive occasion. Gaggles of debs come down from London, as do parents, friends, relatives, and former Oxonians. The girls wear big straw hats and summer frocks and fill the banks of the river Cherwell with color and laughter. Each college has its own boathouse, from the decks and terraces of which all these out of town guests watch the races.

During all this commotion and confusion Mr. Gordon, the President of Magdalen, summoned me to his house.

"Hohenlohe," he said, "we are expecting a former Magdalen undergrad this afternoon, the brother of the Emperor of Japan. I want you to receive him and look after him."

"But Sir, I'm rowing in our eight!"

"Yes, yes, I know. But you can look after him between races. I am relying on you." And with those words I was dismissed.

Prince Chichibu was a younger brother of Emperor

Hirohito. He had studied briefly at Oxford, but had not since returned to visit his old college.

I was on hand to receive him as he alighted from his car when he arrived from London. He was a perfectly charming man. Then I hastened to take him and his retinue to the river, settled them in the best seats on the upper deck of our houseboat, introduced a few notables to him, provided him with tea and cakes, and ran as fast as I could to get into my rowing togs and jump into my number 4 seat in our eight.

After the first race I wiped the sweat from my face and other parts of my body, slid into a pair of white flannels, and raced back to the houseboat and Chichibu. This went on all afternoon, by the end of which I was fit to be carried off on a stretcher. But the Prince enjoyed

Rowing at Oxford, Summer 1935.
The author is fourth from left.

his afternoon tremendously. Before he got back into his Rolls-Royce for the return drive to London, he asked me to sign the small program which all the colleges distributed to guests during eights week. It contained the names of all the crew members. These programs were always handsomely printed; our own program, with the black and white Magdalen crest on its cover, was quite stunning. I obliged, of course, and he departed.

Soon after this carefree, happy time, World War II broke out. Much water flowed under the bridge until, through a twist or two of Fate, I found myself in American uniform treading Japanese soil. It goes without saying that I looked up all my pre-war Japanese friends. Hostilities were forgotten, and we were the

In Japan following the war years with Princess Chichibu at the country estate in Gotemba.

same friends we had always been. Prince Chichibu was one of these. I saw quite a bit of him and his wife, and on one weekend I was invited to their country estate in Gotemba. Right after lunch on Saturday, Prince Chichibu asked me into his study. He went and stood behind his desk, opened the middle drawer, and inserted his hand.

"I give you ten guesses, Franzi," he said. "What do you think I'm holding in my hand?"

"Your Imperial Highness, I haven't a clue. A pen? A pencil? A blotting paper? Some envelopes?"

"Wrong, wrong, wrong," he said, grinning from ear to ear and enjoying himself hugely. And with that he pulled his hand out of the drawer, and in it he held my little rowing program from what truly seemed to be another life!

He had neither lost it, mislaid it, torn it up, or thrown it away—but kept it, quite preciously it seemed, throughout the war. I was immensely touched.

Gügi

So much has already been written about Adolf Hitler, or Schickelgruber as he was known at the time, that I am hesitant to add my little morsel to it. But in the following anecdote he hardly makes an appearance.

It was time for one of the monster National Socialist Party rallies in Nürnberg, which always lasted several days. The city was hermetically closed to all but invited guests, outside of the Nazi participants themselves, of course. Nowadays such guests would be called VIP's. Steph was one of them.

So there she was, on her way to Nürnberg, coming from London. With her were two of her closest friends: a member of parliament, Sir Thomas Moore, and Lady Snowden—both VIP's in their own rights. Sir Thomas because, being an M.P., he was apt to influence his constituents, while the Viscountess Snowden of Ickornshaw, widow of a former Chancellor of the Exchequer, wrote articles in the daily press which the National Socialist leaders hoped to sway in their favor. Be it said in passing: they didn't.

Steph, as the representative of Lord Rothermere, his *Daily Mail* and his thousands of readers, was probably the most desirable VIP of them all.

In Nürnberg, as befitted their position, a de luxe apartment had been reserved for them in the best hotel of the city. They had a balcony and would from there be able to take in the enormous torchlight procession which was always held as a finale to the entire rally.

Gügi Wiedemann, the wife of Hitler's personal adjutant, coming by train from Berlin, was to join them. They were all four close friends and, improbable as it sounds today, even Frau Wiedemann and her husband were ardent anti-Nazis.

Fritz Wiedemann, who had of course been allotted quarters elsewhere, came to see them for a few minutes and said, "Tonight, after the final torchlight parade, when all this monkey-business will be finished, I may

Fritz and Gügi, right, at Castle Leopoldskrow;
at left, Count du Pèrier de Larsan and
Rainier de Monaco's Aunt Pita.

be able to escape for a short while. The Führer will be so surrounded by sycophants that he will not notice my absence. If you like I could drop in on you here for a short while. Of course I shall be dead tired by then. Give me a drop to drink if you will."

And so it was arranged. Everyone was naturally eager to hear what Fritz might me able to tell them of the secrets behind the scene.

When evening came he was as good as his word and showed up in their sitting room where the four others had prepared some champagne and a few canapés. It was rather late; he looked haggard and worn out, but still very tall and handsome in his uniform. Gügi, his wife, before he had time to let himself sink into an armchair, went straight to him, took him by his lapels and propelled him into one of the rooms connecting with the sitting room. It was the bedroom. She then closed the door and even bolted it from the inside—the others could hear it distinctly. They could also hear very distinctly all the noises that followed, and which left no doubt in anyone's mind as to what was going on next door.

Lady Snowden was the first one who found enough breath to open her mouth and speak. She said, "Well!"

Thomas Moore and Steph did not do so well. They were speechless. Even without being a prude this type of conduct left one aghast. But when Gügi Wiedemann reappeared, she was as cool as a cucumber. Fritz meanwhile, quite mortified at his wife's behavior, must have fled out the passage through another door.

"Listen you three," said Gügi, "I know what you think. But let me tell you something. I was a very rich but ugly Swiss girl when I first met Fritz. In spite of my dowry no boy had ever looked at me. Fritz was the first one and has remained the only one in my life to this day. He married me, and in so doing aroused my senses. And now that I am his wife, by golly he has to satisfy them. That is all there is to it. And now let us have a glass of champagne."

In the presence of Schickelgruber at The Eagle's Nest, Hitler's mountain hideaway: Lord Rothemere on the left, Fritz Wiedemann on the right, an interpreter behind them.

Neville Chamberlain

Among our many guests during the summer of '38 at Leopoldskron was a member of the House of Commons. Mr. Cruikshank was the father of a classmate of mine. He had a Scottish constituency and a beautiful estate near Gleneagles. One morning while we were all together at breakfast, the day's papers apprised us of the bombshell news that the British Prime Minister, Mr. Neville Chamberlain, had decided to travel to Berchtesgaden to meet Adolf Hitler in an attempt to prevent the acute political crisis from turning into war.

On reading this, Mr. Cruikshank wondered aloud if it would not be a splendid idea to "surprise the old boy" as he got off the train the following day.

Engineering such a surprise would have been totally out of the question for any mortal at that time: the railway station at the small Bavarian alpine resort where Hitler owned his Eagle's Nest country house was sure to be completely cut off and inaccessible to anyone not having official business there. But as Steph was just then at the peak of her tremendous political influence, and since she did not want to disappoint Mr. Cruikshank in his rather harmless and childish wish, she said, "I'll see what I can do about it," and went off to make a few phone calls.

Steph telephoned to the Obersalzberg and explained

that she had a Scottish M.P. as her house guest and that said house guest would like to greet his countryman the Prime Minister on his arrival the following day. Would this be possible?

Within a very short time the answer was telephoned back. Yes it would.

"Princess Hohenlohe's house guest, Mr. Cruikshank, M.P., would be allowed on the platform, and special tickets to get him through the police cordon would be delivered to the Castle Leopoldskron that same afternoon."

Mr. Cruikshank was very pleased at the ease with which his wish had been granted, but had misgivings about going alone as he spoke no German. He wondered whether Steph would accompany him. She told him that wild horses could not drag her anywhere near that railroad station. She knew that if she put her nose anywhere near it, she would be photographed a thousand times and her picture would be spread all over the papers. And if there was one thing she wished to avoid it was this kind of publicity—or, for that matter, any kind of publicity. Since our move to Leopoldskron she had already been called a Nazi sympathizer, an adventuress, a political busybody, a kept woman, a peddler of influence, and many other epithets that she could have done without. She wanted no part of accompanying Cruikshank to Berchtesgaden. But since this did not solve her guest's linguistic problem, in the end it was I who was chosen to accompany him.

Mr. Cruikshank and I set out the following day in

one of our Mercedes convertibles, driven by our chauffeur, Seiler. Cruikshank was dressed most conservatively in dark city clothes, while I was wearing leather shorts, knee stockings, and a green hat. The day was a scorcher.

There was tremendous excitement not only in and around the railway station, but in all the town of Berchtesgaden. Swastikas and Union Jacks were flying everywhere, and wildly enthusiastic people were thronging the streets or leaning out their windows. It took all of Seiler's very considerable skill to squeeze that enormous car through the mass of humanity and up to the station.

When we had passed the various checkpoints and minute controls, Cruikshank and I suddenly found ourselves all alone on the empty platform of the empty railway station. It was rather a letdown, and it surprised us. But then we heard the approaching train, and before we could utter "House of Commons," it had steamed into the station and we were engulfed in a monstrous mass of people who had traveled along with the British P.M. from Munich, where his plane had landed, and were now streaming out of all the compartments.

There were newspaper correspondents from all over the world, photographers, newsreel cameramen, officials, policemen, plainclothesmen, and men in uniforms. We were completely swamped, and shoved aside in the maelstrom.

Nevertheless, our guest, cool as a cucumber, found his way to the compartment from which Mr.

Chamberlain was seen to be emerging, and there, on that modest country platform, under these extraordinary circumstances, the two Englishmen came eye to eye. It was a study in understatement, and had they not both been so sincere, the scene would have been totally ludicrous.

"Hullo there," said Mr. Chamberlain, looking a bit surprised. "Taking a bit of a vacation, what?"

"Yes, matter of fact, so I am. Staying with the Hohenlohes over in Salzburg. Splendid weather we've been having."

"Ah, yes indeed. Lovely house. Marvelous hostess, I'm told. Never met her myself. But she was a friend of my brother Austen."

"Hard to say. Must see how things go. Well, good-bye old chap. These fellows seem to be waiting for me."

The "fellows" were indeed waiting for him. One of them was Adolf Hitler, rubbing his hands in anticipation on the Obersalzberg. The other one was Joachim von Ribbentrop, the German Foreign Minister, standing beside us.

Five minutes later the little platform was again quite empty. Only Cruikshank and I were still there. It became deliciously quiet as the afternoon sun slanted in through the dusty windows. Seiler could be seen standing outside, waiting for us. We had been part of history for a few exciting minutes. The crowd had now all gone and we drove home.

Lydia Lopokova

The autumn of 1938 was one of great international anxiety. Although World War II did not break out until a year later, every indication seemed to be that it would start at any moment that fall. To compensate for this disturbing state of affairs the weather was glorious, at least in Austria, and stayed warm and sunny far into Indian Summer. I remember riding through the meadows along the Salzach every morning, and having breakfast, lunch and tea out in the garden—bathed in truly southern sunshine.

We stayed at Leopoldskron well into October, and that baroque jewel, built by the Archbishops of Salzburg as a summer residence outside the city walls, and once owned by King Ludwig I of Bavaria, was at its magnificent best.

The house, like all our houses everywhere, was pleasantly full of some of our dearest and closest friends: Prince August Wilhelm of Hohenzollern, "Auwie" to us, was there. Also Leopold Stokowski, Count Frederick Ledebur (ex-husband of Sir Beerbohn Tree's daughter, Iris), Countess du Boisrouvray (the aunt of Prince Rainier of Monaco), Count Felix Schaffgotsch (David Niven's friend, who can be found between the pages of *The Moon is a Balloon*), and many others.

Pop, Steph, Mil and I were all supposed to be in

residence, but such were the demands on our time and lives in those days that we were seldom all there together.

One particular day I was there but my parents and grandparents were not. Pop, the last of the clan, had departed for Budapest the day before. It was tea time. Russinger, the butler, appeared on the terrace, where some guests and I were sitting, to tell me that a lady was on the telephone, calling long distance, asking to speak to Steph.

"Tell her she isn't here," I said, "that she is on a motor trip."

"I did, but she is very insistent. Could you perhaps speak with her?"

There was only one telephone at Leopoldskron and it was most inconveniently located in a cubicle off the main hall. Leaving my tea and all the others, I went inside. The voice at the other end of the line sounded very unhappy. It was Lady Keynes, the former Russian ballerina Lopokova, wife of the distinguished British economist John Maynard Keynes. She was calling from Munich. I told her who I was and said that Steph was away. Was there a message I could deliver on her return?

"No you can't," said Lady Keynes. "The matter is very urgent. Your mother, bless her, is the only one of my friends, the only intelligent woman I know in this world, whose judgment I trust implicitly. No one is ever as well informed as she. I am here in Munich on the advice of my London physician. I'm to undergo a very delicate and dangerous operation. The German surgeon to whom I was recommended is the greatest specialist in his field, and I would not hesitate to enter the clinic at once if it weren't for the political situation. If war breaks out I would be cut off from my husband and unable to return to England for the duration."

"Lady Keynes," I replied, "may I call you back? I will see if I can locate my mother."

"Certainly, my child. But hurry. I am a very sick woman. I shall be here in my hotel room awaiting your call."

Immediately after hanging up I tried the Villa d'Este in Como, then the Danieli in Venice, and several other places where I thought my globe-trotting mother might be. But I failed to locate her anywhere. Occasionally, when Steph had a surfeit of family life, she would get in her car and disappear without saying where she was going.

Returning to my interrupted tea on the terrace, I said to the assembled company, "It was Lord Keynes' wife. She wanted Steph to tell her if there's going to be a war before she decides on major surgery in Munich."

"Certainly there won't be a war," said Pita du Boisrouvray indignantly. "Look at the weather. Glorious! Unless he's a fool, Hitler will want to harvest the last crop before he starts anything serious."

"If there is going to be a war," chimed in Princess Irena Obolensky, whose brother Alexander was in training with the R.A.F., "Alec would certainly have told me."

"There simply can't be a war," said Diana Duval,

the most frivolous of us all, "before I've had a date with Ezio Pinza. That man is divine. Do you remember him in those tights in *Don Giovanni?*"

And so it went all around the table, each one of them giving a silly opinion. Our joie de vivre, youth, or possibly just plain obtuseness, were such that I marched back to the phone, called Lady Keynes, and said, "I didn't reach my mother, but there will be no war. You can go ahead and have your operation."

And there wasn't. And she did. And was grateful forever after.

The Gestapo and I

After ten years of one of the most successful collaborations on Fleet Street, the professional partnership between Steph and her employer suddenly came to an end. Lord Rothermere retired from the newspaper and handed over the chairmanship of the *Daily Mail* to his son, the Hon. Esmond Harmsworth. As a result of this move, Steph was dropped without warning from one day to the next. She retaliated by preparing a lawsuit for breach of contract.

In Austria the never-ending summer had turned into one of the coldest winters on record. The lake at Leopoldskron froze over, and when we all returned there for the Christmas and New Year's holidays, we were able to skate and curl right in front of our own windows. Again the house was full to bursting with guests—among them the nephew of the Nizam of Hyderabad, reputedly the richest man on earth in those days before the discovery of oil around the Persian Gulf.

When the holidays were over everyone except I departed once more. A friend, Count Ludwig Platz, had lent me his alpine chalet, and I went there to ski with a girlfriend, Irena Obolensky. But the snow fell in such quantities, day after day, that we were soon snowed in. Skiing was quite out of the question. When the snowfall finally subsided, it was time for us to return to Salzburg. A sleigh drove us to the nearest railroad station, but due to weather conditions all trains were many hours late. We arrived in Salzburg in the middle of the night, and rather than waking the servants at such an hour, we put up at the Österreichischer Hof until the following morning. The next day I called our housekeeper, Frau Gwinner, to let her know we were back. I could tell from her strained voice that something was amiss.

"Where are you?" she whispered.

"Here in Salzburg, at the Österreichischer Hof."

"Don't leave the hotel," she said rapidly and out of breath. "I'll be there within half an hour. I'll bring Josef."

Josef was my valet. I could not figure out why she wanted to bring him, but knowing how intelligent she was I realized there must be a good reason. In those days one's antennae were sensitive and one expected the unexpected daily.

I told Irena of the curious conversation I'd had with Frau Gwinner, and she too was immediately alarmed. When Frau Gwinner and Josef arrived, I saw that they had brought a goodly number of my suitcases with them. All of them were full and contained as many of my clothes and belongings as they had managed to pack in such a hurry. Without wasting a moment on preliminaries, Frau Gwinner began her story.

"Just before you called, we had the visit of three government officials, members of the Nazi party. They asked if anyone of the family were in residence. I said that everyone was away. I said nothing about you skiing here in the Alps. But fortunately they did not ask me. Then they informed me that they were acting on orders from Berlin. The castle was being confiscated as of today, and seals were to be put on everything."

When she finished she broke down in tears, and I consoled her. She and Josef and Irena and I all embraced and shook hands, but at the door Frau Gwinner turned back, came back to me and took me in her arms. Josef also turned back and kissed my hand, wetting it with his tears. Then the two were gone.

After their departure I immediately got on the phone to Steph in London. Calls from Germany to other countries were very easy to put through because so few people dared to call abroad. The lines were never busy. I reached Steph in no time at all. She was sitting in her bath, the telephone by her side—a very dangerous habit of which she was never cured.

"Weriand," I said, using one of my seven Christian names, "is experiencing a little difficulty. He can't go to his parents' house. The doors are locked."

Steph, who was brighter than the Kohinoor diamond and understood everything before one had finished one's sentence, did not lose her cool for a second.

"I'm sorry to hear that," she replied. "Tell him that if he came to see me it would be helpful. But meanwhile he should try to settle at the Continental in Munich, today!"

The "today" was ominous, and although I am not

as bright as the Kohinoor diamond—far from it—I understood at once. I told her I would give Weriand the message if I ran across him, and then hung up.

Following this, Irena and I went into a huddle and came up with this plan: Being the one whose name was Hohenlohe, it was I and not she who was in danger. I'd have to leave for Munich immediately. If Steph had said the Continental, there was surely a reason for it. (It turned out there was; she knew and could trust and at a pinch also bribe its porter.) So I would go to that hotel and not the Regina or the Vier Jahreszeiten. But Irena could not come with me because, being a white Russian, she traveled under a Nansen passport and needed to have it stamped and validated before she could leave the "Ostmark." We were certain, however, that this would not take her more than two days and that she could then join me in Munich. Also, it was wiser for me not to be seen traveling with my little Skye terrier Katia, as she too was well known. For years we had owned many Skye terriers. They had become a trademark of ours. Irena would have to keep her.

I arrived in Munich that night and the porter at the Continental told me there had been a call for me from London. I returned the call and told Steph that I had given Weriand her message and he would be happy to visit her in England. There was only one difficulty. Weriand had plenty of Reichsmark but, being a foreigner, was not allowed to use these to buy a railway ticket for outside the country. Steph said she would solve this problem somehow, but in the meantime Weriand had better get himself a French transit visa.

The next day my first errand was to call at the French Consulate and apply for that visa. I filled out all the forms, had myself photographed, paid my dues, and was told to wait.

"You will be notified in time."

Consulates are never in a very great hurry, and this one was no exception. Every day I called there to see where matters stood, only to be told "perhaps tomorrow."

I had nothing at all to do in Munich, and time dragged on. Irena was still in Salzburg—her papers, too, were more difficult to obtain than anticipated. The snow never let up and the city of Munich was like a citadel of Outer Siberia. My room was poorly heated. Fortunately, thanks to Josef and Frau Gwinner, I had practically everything I owned with me—including plenty of warm clothes. But I could not sit in my room all day, and as for the hotel lobby, I avoided it as much as possible.

After a day or two I noticed that whenever I left the hotel, having walked through the lobby at a brisk pace, a man I had no difficulty recognizing after the second time would be loitering in front. Hardly would I set out in whatever direction when he would do the same. What made this man unbelievably ludicrous was the fact that, despite the mountains of snow which mechanical snow shovels were clearing away daily as best they could, he was pushing, of all things, a bicycle!

He also never bothered to change his clothes, and wore the same cap and breeches each time I saw him. There was no doubt in my mind that he was from the Gestapo. They must, quite obviously, have held my powers of observation in low esteem, to have me tailed for so many days running by so undisguised a "trailer."

Since I had nothing to do all day, I usually made a round of the sweet shops in search of marshmallows to assuage my sweet tooth. These were, unaccountably, in sugar-rationed Germany, still available—albeit not in many stores. Wherever I entered, the "trailer" would stop in front, bicycle in hand, to contemplate the window displays of marzipans and gumdrops.

In the afternoons my trailing companion was a woman. She too never varied. She was tall and gaunt and had "police matron" written all over her. I am glad to be able to say that I outsmarted her every time. Whenever I had taken her for a good long walk, I would head for a cinema. As soon as I had entered the darkened auditorium, I would stand right by the door and not budge. By the time she also came through the door, while her eyes were still unadjusted to the dark, I would immediately slip out. She never caught on.

Finally it all came to an end. I got my visa and left for Paris and London. Peace was behind us. War loomed ahead.

The fainting deb

Another occasion. Another party. I was now in my mid-teens. This one was a hunt ball in an English country house. Some of the girls had already made their debut that season and had come down from London. But most of them were local belles still waiting to be presented at court—all fresh from finishing school.

The band struck up a waltz. As a Viennese I considered myself honor-bound to not sit this one out, although my starched shirt and white tie were already wilting. Walking up to a very pretty girl totally unknown to me, I asked her to dance. She accepted. We were off. Her conversation was less than monosyllabic. It was nil. She was definitely not one of the more sophisticated London crew.

After awhile I inquired if waltzing made her giddy and if she wanted me to reverse. Fortunately she said no, for I am very bad at reversing, despite all that Viennese blood coursing through my veins. The "no" she uttered was the second word she had spoken. The first being "yes" when I had invited her to dance.

We waltzed on. The band didn't seem to know how to stop. On and on they played. Round and round, right, right, right, we went on waltzing.

"Are you quite sure," I asked again, "that this won't make you dizzy?"

"Oh no, certainly not," she replied. Four more words. Except that she didn't get to the end of them when, zonk, down she went for the count of ten.

What do the etiquette books say you're to do when an unknown girl faints dead away in your arms? The other couples around us went right on dancing. No one had noticed. The prone white form of my deb on the floor, at my feet, did not cause a ripple. She had slid out of my arms in a mass of organdy. There is mighty little one can do in such a situation except pick up the victim and carry her out, saying "Sorry" or "Beg pardon" to those you bump into on the way. It's what I did, while the band went right on playing. Were they never going to stop?

There was no one in the hall outside the ballroom. No host, no hostess, no fellow guests, no servants. I could have done with a little brandy to pour down her throat, or may be some old-fashioned smelling salts. Burnt feathers, people said, were very helpful when held under the nose. In my despair, finding no one, and still carrying that dead weight in my arms, I made for the stairs and carried her to the first floor landing. Surely, I thought, there must be help of some sort somewhere in this house! Perhaps in these upper regions there would be an attendant or a child of the house leaning over the bannisters. But there was no one.

The first door I came upon led to a bedroom. It stood ajar. I kicked it wide open. Some coats lay strewn on the bed. I plunked my unconscious debbie on top of them and was just going to get some cold water to sprinkle on her face, when she opened her eyes. Taking one frightened look at me standing by the bed on which she was lying, and misconstruing the situation entirely, she let out a shriek and ran from the room.

I never saw her again.

Serves me right for thinking I had to waltz when I could have sat that one out.

Clare Luce and Bernard Shaw

We were a small party waiting to go in to lunch at the Ritz in London. Only one guest was still missing: Clare Luce. Finally, hungry and impatient, our host, Professor Rudolph Kommer, said, "Maybe she's forgotten. Let's go in without her."

Mrs. Luce hadn't forgotten and did show up, though very late.

"You must forgive me," she said. "I came straight from the house of Bernard Shaw. I had wanted to meet him all my life, and finally it could be arranged. I told him that as an author (her immensely popular *The Women* had just been published) I felt that he was completely responsible for me, to which he replied, 'What did you say that your mother's name was?'"

Marlene

On Bastille Day of 1939, three months before the outbreak of World War II, the city of Paris, as it always did on its national holiday, offered a series of outdoor performances, free of charge, to its several million inhabitants. These were held on the terrace of Trocadero, under the Eiffel Tower, on the Place de la Bastille, and on the Opera Square.

I was with a group of people in Miss Hoytie Wiborg's apartment around cocktail time. It was a chic, international, brittle crowd. We decided on the spur of the moment to have dinner at the Café de la Paix, and watch the show in front of the Opera from there. Reservations were made for a table of twelve in one of the dining rooms of that world-famous café, upstairs near the windows, on the side facing the outdoor stage. From there we had a wonderful, unimpeded view of the proceedings, above the heads of the milling crowds.

The main attraction below was to be Marlene Dietrich, and the cynical circle of cosmopolites I was with was speculating that she would make a fool of herself. They were, in fact, looking forward to it with glee—like the Roman populace under Nero, hoping the gladiators would be eaten up by the lions.

An immense stage had been erected for Marlene and the other artists to perform on. It stretched the entire length of Opera Square, and was as bare and uninviting as a stage can possibly be: no backdrop, no scenery, no curtain in front, no spotlights—not even a few potted palms to relieve its nakedness. This was the battleground on which the famous star was expected to go down in flames. The atmosphere in the air was quite definitely hostile. With most Frenchmen expecting war against Germany to break out at any moment, the timing was bad for a German actress to be singing on, of all days, the 14th of July! You could very palpably feel the public's animosity.

Marlene, in those days, was not yet the nightclub and theatre performer she subsequently became with such resounding success. It was years before her appearances at the Café de Paris in London, or her one-woman shows at Las Vegas and all over the world. What, these people were asking themselves, was this Boche film actress going to do up there? Would she dance? Juggle? Do card tricks? No one knew. Her *Blue Angel* film success was far behind—ten years to be precise—so there had been time for the general public to forget that she was not only a film star, but a very clever diseuse as well.

When it finally grew dark enough for the show to begin, and after a few minor introductory acts, Marlene came on. There was a hush in that enormous square and you could hear the proverbial pin dropping. Everyone—especially my hard-boiled socialites—expected her to make a typical movie star entrance. We all "knew" that she would appear in an evening gown;

whoever heard of appearing in anything else? And of course, regardless of the evening's warmth, she would be wrapped in furs. Perhaps white fox with possibly a spray of orchids at the shoulder. Jewels also; yes, naturally, she would be wearing jewels. There would be glitter, lots of glitter—a sequined dress, tight-fitting and split to the knee!

While all these catty thoughts were crossing everyone's mind, a slim girl, blonde and pretty and terribly young, suddenly skipped up the steps at one far end of the stage. No one helped her. No one bowed.

The petite amie—Marlene Dietrich.

No one introduced her. She was left strictly unassisted, completely on her own, to deal with that frightful distance between those wobbly wooden steps and the center of the huge stage where a lone microphone had been set up. The slim, golden girl was wearing a little white street dress, short and swingy and deceptively simple. And that was all she had on. No hat, no veil, no gloves, no flowers, no trailing chiffon handkerchief, not a single jewel.

As she started to cross the stage, a gasp went through the audience. "Mais cest elle! C'est Marlene!

She dealt with the tricky distance between herself and the microphone in such masterly fashion that it wrought admiration from everyone before she ever reached it. There was complete confidence in that walk but not a spark of arrogance. This was not the mincing gait of a movie queen. these were the assured steps of a young woman secure in her good looks and totally unaware that anyone in that arena might possibly be hostile to her. She exuded confidence and immediately established a warm contact with the populace of Paris. When she reached center stage, without any introductory speech by an M.C., she started to sing—in French, and without the trace of an accent.

Marlene the German film star was standing there, in the middle of Paris, in her little white dress (which even if it had been made, as it most probably was, by one of the great, expensive maisons de couture, looked so simple), and she held everyone in the palm of her hand. She had chosen to begin with "La Madelon," the song most certainly designed to tug at the heartstrings of that most patriotic nation. Long before she reached the end, the battle was won! They were all on her side. Perhaps she had won them over before ever opening her mouth.

To every man she was the picture of the "petite amie" whom he could take to a bal musette without constraint. To every girl she seemed just like herself. that little white dress was so easy to copy, or so they all thought. There was nothing to it. "I can look like that any day, myself," they mused. Many a sewing machine must have been set in motion the very next day, trying to turn out copies of Marlene's deceptively simple little dress.

When the show was over, and many encores had been sung, the roaring, screaming, applauding public did not want to let her go. Marlene had to be whisked through an underground passage from the opera to the Café de la Paix where her car was waiting to take her to her next singing appointment that evening. But as the crowd spotted her leaving the Café de la Paix, people threw themselves in front of the automobile so that her chauffeur was unable to drive. It took the police to set her free. Had it still been the days of the horse and buggy, they would have unhitched them and drawn her carriage themselves.

That is what I call Showmanship with a capital S!

War

When war broke out I was on the high seas heading for New York. The thought that this war would finally hit us had never really sunk into my skull, although Lord knows it had been smoldering for a long enough time. But far more pressing to me was an urge to flee the family after the shattering row we'd had at Le Touquet between tennis in the morning and golf in the afternoon.

I had decided there and then, on the second green, to run away from home—and today I am ashamed to admit it for running away should be done, if at all, between the ages of eleven and twelve, no more. Eleven to twelve I wasn't. I wanted to show the world that I could get along without my powerful and influential family, make my own living, stand on my own two feet, and a few more heroic platitudes. But first I had to reach America, the country of unlimited possibilities (with borrowed money, for my allowance had been cut off).

In those days, American immigration laws required every foreigner to arrive with a minimum of $2,000 on his person, to ensure that he would not become a charge of the state. My school chum Paddy Cruikshank anteed this sum. On arrival in New York I immediately returned it to him, so that I was $2,000 poorer on the very second day. My goal was California, the land of milk and honey, where it was quite clear to me that William Randolph Hearst, who had been so hospitable to me on two previous visits, would offer me a job on one of his numerous papers.

I had some very good friends in Hollywood, the Victor Varconis. Victor was a film star. Without doubt I could stay with them for a while in the beginning.

After a very few days in New York, at a very different type of hotel from the Waldorf Astoria where I had stayed before, I set out for Los Angeles by Greyhound Bus. To the Varconis I sent a letter giving them the day and time of my arrival. The taxi from the downtown bus terminal to the Varconi house in the Outpost was ruinously expensive, but quite unavoidable since there had been no one to meet me at the gate when my bus pulled in.

When the door of the house was opened to me, after I had pressed the buzzer twice, I was struck a ghastly blow. The woman who stood there was neither Mrs. Varconi nor her daughter, with whom I had enjoyed a slight flirtation. This lady spoke with a lovely British accent and inquired what I wanted.

"The Victor Varconis."

"I'm sorry—they no longer live here. They moved away six months ago."

"I felt the blood draining from my face. There was nothing else to do but apologize, turn on my heels, and return to my taxi which fortunately had not yet left. I told the driver to take me to a very inexpensive hotel, and he did. It was at the corner of Hollywood Boulevard and Western Avenue, in a tough neighborhood with the highest crime rate in the entire city.

Some years later I was attending a cocktail party when one of the guests came up to me. "Aren't you the young man who once came to my house looking for the Victor Varconis?" she asked, in that same lovely British voice. I acknowledged that I was.

"D'you know," she continued, "your face, your poor, stricken face as I told you the Varconis no longer lived in that house, has pursued me for years. My husband is an actor. He was away on location. The house is large, and I could so easily have taken you in. But when I thought of this and ran back to the door your taxi was already rounding the bend and driving downhill . . . "

Hollywood

I now entered upon what was the poorest of all my breadless days. But it is at such times that one can judge the true kindness of one's friends. And friends I had aplenty—all of them new ones.

On leaving my home and family in London—forever, I thought, after the monumental fight which made me determine to run away—I entrusted the secret of my destination to no one except one girl with whom I was very close at the time. I made her swear on a stack of Bibles that she would not give away my secret to anyone, especially the family, with whom she was on very good terms. But I had not reckoned with the fact that my family is strong, very strong, and the girl was weak, very weak. In a very short time they squeezed my secret out of her among an avalanche of tears. Now everyone knew that I had sailed for America.

Meanwhile, I had very quickly moved from the fleabag hotel at which my taxi driver had deposited me and into the then still very clean and proper Hollywood YMCA.

My meals were taken once a day, on every second day. I gulped them down in the middle of the day so that they would count for breakfast, lunch and dinner all at once. This single meal was always a blue plate special at some drugstore and cost—oh blessed days!—

$1 exactly. That modest sum even included a choice of soft drink. The rest of the time I did not eat at all, and when I felt hungry I would go to a water fountain and drink. This filled me up. Yet, on the other end of the scale, among the very rich people I knew were Mr. and Mrs. Keith Spalding, manufacturers of Spalding tennis racquets and other assorted sporting goods. They were old guard and lived in Pasadena at the very select Huntington Hotel, stronghold of conservatism, where they owned a large bungalow on the grounds. They also owned an equally large yacht with a crew of fourteen, that they kept in San Pedro Harbor. The Spaldings were elderly people who led a quiet life, and they never ever asked anyone aboard this splendid yacht. They were both dedicated to fishing, and kept the yacht for this purpose. Mrs. Spalding, though an invalid confined to a wheelchair, was the champion deep sea fisherman of Southern California!

For me the Spaldings broke their rule! I was invited to go sailing and fishing with them. Their liveried chauffeur came in a long car to pick me up at the modest YMCA, and drove me to San Pedro where the yacht was berthed. The Spaldings were already aboard and we sailed off immediately. Our days on the Pacific Ocean always followed the same pattern. Soon after breakfast Mrs. Spalding in her wheelchair would be lowered into a launch and go off with a few sailors by herself. Keith Spalding and I and a few more sailors came next, and we would go off in another direction.

At night, after an outstanding dinner prepared by the French chef they kept aboard, partaken by us in evening clothes, I would be set to catching flying fish with a net and electric light. These served as bait for the next day's deep sea fishing.

Sometimes, in the afternoons, I was encouraged to go aquaplaning behind the speedboat which was lowered for me alone.

My one dollar blue plate specials tasted a bit meagre after that luxury interlude.

Keith Spalding instructed his lawyer, Mr. George Farrand, to get me put on a proper quota number waiting list, so that I could legally accept a job. I had arrived in America on a visitor's visa, and was therefore forbidden by law to take on remunerated employment.

Mr. Farrand was no specialist in immigration matters, but he accepted the assignment with optimism and was quite certain that within a short time he would succeed. Meanwhile, he invited me to his home on Windsor Boulevard, in a select neighborhood of Los Angeles. I met his wife and two sons, all of whom could not have been nicer to me. Knowing the frightful poverty in which I was living, they found the most tactful, elegant way of letting a little money pass into my pockets. They asked me to give them French conversation lessons, which they really didn't need. Two evenings a week a liveried driver in a big car would come and pick me up at the Y and drive me to Windsor Boulevard, where we first settled down to a good dinner before beginning with the lessons. I am sure it was thanks to the Farrand's kindness that I did not quite starve to death during that period.

But alas, as far as my visa went, Mr. Farrand got nowhere. I remained a visitor on a visitor's visa.

From William Randolph Hearst, to whom I had written on arrival, hoping he could find employment for me on one of his numerous papers, and that his political clout could break the stalemate of my visa situation, I heard nothing.

My sister Elisabeth

As compensation for what was for me so disastrous an autumn and winter, the weather in Southern California was wonderful. One warm and balmy Sunday a bunch of us fellows from the Y drove to Santa Monica in someone's old jalopy. We went to the beach primarily to play ball. None of us had any money, but made up for our lack with lots of zip, voom and pep.

A group of men and one girl sat on the sand next to where we left our belongings. They all spoke French, and pretty soon I got to talking with them. It turned out that all were either waiters or barmen in different hotels and restaurants. The girl was the wife of one of them, or so she said. She was German, and her name was Elisabeth. Before we all broke up to drive back to Hollywood I gave her my name and telephone number, and that evening she called and asked me to her apartment for dinner. Her fellow, the "husband," had gone off to work and she was alone.

Elisabeth made me a very good home-cooked dinner, and extracted my story from me while we ate. By the time we had reached dessert she had decided that all this business of a visitor's visa was ridiculous, and that she would find me a job where no one would be any the wiser. We set out in her car about ten, and hit a considerable number of bars and night spots. From the way she was greeted everywhere, I could tell that she was very well known and very well liked in this midnight world of which I knew nothing. Right from the start she informed me that it would make matters easier if she said I was her kid brother recently arrived from Germany.

To my utter amazement, I was offered jobs by many of her chums right from the start of our tour. But Elisabeth, who judged them to be unworthy of my talents, made discreet "no" signs with her head. One man, quite certainly a minor gangster, wished to employ me to make the rounds of Hollywood every morning and gather the contents of the one-armed bandits he owned here and there. My sister Elisabeth's "no" shake was very emphatic.

Finally, in the wee hours of the morning, we found ourselves in a night spot called "The Sphinx" on the Sunset Strip. By that late hour it was almost empty, but sitting on a barstool was a deadly drunk Englishman with his bodyguard, who was sober. Elisabeth knew them both and sat herself down next to the lush. He was very well dressed, though in rumpled condition, and by his speech—such as was still capable of coming out of his mouth—it was obvious that he was well educated and a gentleman. Elisabeth whispered his story into my ear: he was a well-known, distinguished scenario writer, much sought after by the studios, and in a very substantial income bracket. He had a wife and a home, and most of the time led a perfectly respectable sober life. But when the urge hit him to go out on the town, he called his bodyguard and stayed drunk for an entire weekend. For that purpose, he had an apartment at the Roosevelt Hotel, and never returned to his home and wife until he had completely sobered up.

Before long the Englishman offered to put me on his payroll, so Elisabeth and I stayed with him until The Sphinx turned us out, around six in the morning. My sister no longer had a reason to shake her head. She was happy for me. We followed the bodyguard who drove ahead to the Roosevelt Hotel. Once upstairs in his apartment, the Englishman retired to his bedroom, leaving guard, sister and me in the living room to order breakfast. His reappearance took a long time. He had showered, shaved, and changed his bedraggled clothes. His hair was neatly combed. His shoes were shined. His shirt was snow white. In other words, he was a new man. And after a few cups of strong black coffee he was also perfectly sober and repeated his offer to employ me right away, to type his scenarios. I almost whooped with joy!

After returning to the Y to clean up and change my clothes, I immediately took a bus downtown to Mr. Farrand's office. I told him the good news and he tried even harder to get me that coveted quota number. But none of his efforts were to any avail. I never got it—not then, and not later.

The daily bread

When I think of all the things I have already done in life to earn a living it makes me dizzy. It started very early in the Paris apartment when I was of an age where one wears out one's clothes at a fast clip. I considered it very wasteful that these should always be given away to the Salvation Army or the Catholic Church. All those shirts and pants and shoes and socks that went down the drain, so to speak, so anonymously. Surely, I thought, there must be a better answer! And I found it in the person of Madame Crist. (It was probably Ernst who found her for me.) She came to our apartment whenever I called her, and bought everything I offered. My family was mortified at this mercenary streak in me, and Madame Crist had to use the back stairs.

At the Collège de Normandie I had a small roulette wheel in my desk. As is well known, the odds are always in favor of the banker and against the gamblers. Therefore, I was the banker. I won quite regularly. With the proceeds I enticed the young yokel who was the servant on my floor, and who brought us hot water with which to wash every morning, to buy me some eggs in Montcauvaire, the nearest village, which I whipped into meringue and ate with the addition of a little purloined sugar from the dining hall.

In my last term, before I left school with, thank

Allah, my baccalaureate degree in hand, I held an auction at which were sold my bicycle, canoe, the pictures on the walls of my room, the roulette wheel, and a delirious photograph of Marlene Dietrich, with long stretched out legs, and autographed in . . . white ink! It had been the envy of all my housemates ever since I'd received it.

When I reached Oxford, immediately after these commercial transactions, I got to write on not one but two columns on two rival papers, the *Cherwell* and the *Isis*. Very soon thereafter came the picture exhibition that I have related in an earlier chapter.

When war broke out and I had run away from home, Pop succeeded in making me an American correspondent of the Hungarian pictorial *Szinházy Elet*. They paid very little, but anything in those days was welcome. This job came to an end when I was arrested and locked up on Ellis Island.

And all these preliminaries were followed by work as a mechanic, a carpenter, a teacher, a model, a pin boy in a bowling alley, a baker, a book wrapper-upper, a travel agent, an interpreter, a typist, a soldier, a sailor, a banker, a clothing manufacturer, a journalist, an author, and a lecturer.

The Bavarian bed

Now at last I was under William Randolph Hearst's roof. Under one of his many roofs, I should rightly say. I was in Wyntoon, that fabulous place so few people know of, in the northern part of California, at the foot of Mount Shasta. It was because of hope in my heart that Mr. Hearst, who had been so kind and hospitable to me on my last foray to California, would find employment for me on one of his numerous papers, that I had traveled far, from New York to California, and before that from London to New York. One might say that it was because of this hope that I had run away from home. I had not realized that it would be impossible for Mr. Hearst to hire me, since I was a visitor to the United States without a work visa.

Here I was, then, in Wyntoon, but not up and about with the other guests. I was in bed with the worst cold, influenza, or maybe pneumonia, that I had ever had. And the bed I was in was undoubtedly the least comfortable bed to be ill in of all the beds in the all the world. It was huge, very beautiful and antique. It was Bavarian. Hearst and his lady-in-residence, adorable Marion Davies, had picked it up on one of their travels in Germany. It was intricately carved and one could not lean on its back for fear of cutting a gash in one's head. It was also as long as it was wide, six foot by six foot, and if you lay in its middle there were acres of icy sheet on either side of you, and you could not reach the night tables. But as I shook and trembled and sneezed and wheezed, hoping for a quick death to deliver me from this illness, I did not try to reach the night tables. All the houses in Wyntoon, mostly designed and decorated by Willy Pogany, had names. Mine on that frightful occasion was Rier House. The time before I had been put in Cinderella House. When I opened my eyes I could see the lovely landscape of huge trees, reminiscent of the forests of Bavaria, only bigger and better. An ice cold river flowed right by my window, and people could fish from the balcony.

Wyntoon was so large that for every meal partaken with W.R. and Marion and all the guests at the main house, one had to ring for a car to pick you up and drive you there. I, of course, was brought my meals on trays. Nobody came to see me. Mr. Hearst was known to be terrified of infection, so nobody dared approach my sickbed. One guest, however, dared slip in to see me every day, bringing me newspapers, candy, friendship and chitchat. As Hearst owned the *Daily American, Town and Country, Harper's Bazaar* and dozens of other dailies and periodicals, one was never lacking in anything to read. This Friend, Mexican born Princess Conchita Pignatelli, was my only contact with the world of the living. She was a columnist on one of Hearst's papers.

But then one day, after shivering and being hot and cold in turns for about a week, a miracle happened:

Marion herself appeared in my room and sat down on my huge bed. Now Marion, although she was an actress, had a heart-breaking stutter which made her even more appealing.

"Hu, hu, honey" she said, "ah, ah, are you any bet, better?"

"Frankly Marion, no, I'm not. Why do you ask?"

"Be, be, because for this, this bed, we only have one pair of sheets."

The death of Valentino

For many years, Marion Davies entertained her guests with the story of Pola Negri's return from the East Coast following the death of screen idol Rudolph Valentino, with whom Pola had a sizzling love affair.

Although the term "vamp" was coined for actress Theda Bara, no siren of the silver screen was ever more vampish than Pola Negri. While Theda, a quiet housewife in private life, took her vamping with a grain of salt, Pola was always dead serious about it. This heavy-lidded seductress with the heaving bosom carried the vamp style into her home and everywhere she went. A native of Poland, her acting career gained prominence when she moved to pre-Hitler Berlin and began working for the immensely talented Ernst Lubitsch at UFA Studios.

Charlie Chaplin, who happened to be visiting Germany at the time, met Pola and fell in love with her. Through his influence, Pola—and also Lubitsch—left Germany for America, and settled in Hollywood. Pola's arrival in the American film capital was greeted with much ballyhoo and her success was immediate, although her films were never among the top money makers. Few of her scripts allowed Pola to enjoy a happy end. She was torn by destiny (usually in satin and pearls), abandoned (in chinchilla), disdained (in a royal castle), misunderstood (with aigrettes in her hair), enslaved (with many diamond bracelets dangling from her wrist). She was put under contract to Paramount, where the reigning movie queen was Gloria Swanson. Stories of their feud kept the gossip columns filled for years; some of them true, most of them invented.

Around 1925 this consummate vamp fell in love once more—with dashing Rudolph Valentino. Like her romance with Chaplin, this one was also a sizzler, but short-lived, and finally tragic. Valentino died in the summer of 1926 at the age of 32 in New York City, while Pola was in Hollywood making a movie. In a well-publicized dash across the continent—by train, of course, those days being pre-transcontinental flight—Pola made the most of the opportunity but arrived too late. She wore black, and heavy veils, cried a lot, gave out many interviews, and altogether didn't miss a single trick to further her career.

After Pola's three-day trip to Rudy's deathbed, there was the three-day return trip to Hollywood, where again all her swoons and statements to the press made headlines. She may have cared for Valentino quite genuinely, but wasn't going to let that stand in her way of making the most of his passing.

It was Marion Davies who met Pola's train upon its arrival in Pasadena. Alighting from her luxurious drawing room compartment, Pola wanted to be taken, "First of all, to Falcon's Lair," Valentino's house on top of one of Hollywood's highest hills. Miss Davies obliged and instructed her chauffeur accordingly.

When the Rolls-Royce stopped in front of Falcon's Lair, Pola made straight for Rudy's bedroom, "To commune with his spirit alone." Waiting considerately outside the door, Marion was startled to hear an ominous, heavy thump. Rushing inside, she found Pola stretched out cold in an artistic heap on the floor.

"Quick, Mario," Miss Davies called to the butler, whom she knew well from past visits. "Bring brandy! Miss Negri has fainted."

"There is no brandy in the house, Miss Davies" replied Mario. "But we do have some champagne."

"Bring that," said Marion. "We must revive her."

Mario brought the champagne, and they poured some drops between Pola's pale, parted lips. But her reaction was unexpected. Opening one eye and spitting out the champagne, she exclaimed, "Phew. Filthy! *Italian.*"

(This being the era of Prohibition, French champagne was unobtainable—even through the best bootleggers.)

Working at this and working at that

After returning to Hollywood from William Randolph Hearst's luxurious Wyntoon, it was back to the YMCA and one meal every second day. That incredibly kind couple, Mr. and Mrs. George Farrand, did me the immense kindness of pretending that they wanted me to continue giving them French conversation lessons, and the lessons went on as before: their car and chauffeur were sent to fetch me and take me to dinner at their house. The lessons, such as they were, were given after dessert, with coffee in their living room, and generously paid for.

Meanwhile, over in London, Steph had lost a spectacular lawsuit which she had unwisely waged against her all-powerful former employer, Harold Harmsworth, Viscount Rothermere. The tabloids on both sides of the Atlantic wrote about her defeat for weeks thereafter, in enormous front page headlines. She then went to New York, where a staggering number of publishers had made her very substantial offers for her memoirs—which in the end she never wrote! A great pity, as it would have put a great deal of money in her coffers.

Steph moved into the Waldorf Astoria and was pursued by the press and photographers night and day. When on one occasion one of them came flashing his bulbs at her while she was sitting in her bathtub (how he got in she never found out), she moved to the Plaza, not yet owned by Conrad Hilton and his future wife Zsa Zsa Gábor.

The quarrel between myself and my family, which had caused me to run off to America in the first place, was now completely patched up. Even Pop, way back in distant Budapest, cooperated and had me appointed American correspondent to the Hungarian magazine *Szinházy Élet*. Since my Hungarian was still more than shaky, I wrote my weekly articles in English, sometimes in German, and my stepmother, "Aunt" Ella, translated them when they arrived in the Hungarian capital.

Grandmother Mil then stepped in and decided that a foreign correspondent had better know what the whole game was about. I was enrolled in a journalism class at Stanford University for a short but very happy interlude in my life. The student body of Stanford in those days counted 5,000 boys and a very small sprinkling of girls. Today Stanford has 20,000 students!

But after Stanford I struck another low. The family was then deep into its own troubles. The Hohenlohes were hounded by such s.o.b.'s as Walter Winchell, Robert Ruark, J. Edgar Hoover, attorney general Francis Biddle, and even, I am sorry to say, President Franklin Roosevelt. Of all this I have written in another book, so I shall not repeat it. But it was no time for me to impose my own troubles on theirs. I finished my condensed courses at Stanford and returned to New York, where I took on two simultaneous jobs: modeling for the Harry Conover agency in the daytime, and wrapping books a the Book-of-the-Month-Club at night. Oh, the fatigue! Modeling—very often for high fashion magazines—took up all day every day. But my work at the Book-of-the-Month-Club started promptly at 5 p.m. We wrapped books from 5 to 9 p.m., when we got an hour off for a meal that the club called, most incongruously, "lunch." The second half of our shift stretched interminably from 10 p.m. to 2 a.m. By that time my feet would hardly carry me. Such was my fatigue that I would cross Central Park to shorten the trip to my room at the Y on the west side of Manhattan— indifferent to the possibility of getting mugged, held up, raped or murdered. By 8 a.m. I had to be up again and ready for all the photographers, hopefully looking fresh as dew. What a life!

In my grandmother's garden in Alexandria,
Virginia, shortly before my arrest by the
F.B.I. and two years behind barbed wire.

Arrested

Three men stared suspiciously at me as they flashed a badge and announced, "We are from the FBI and have come with orders to apprehend you."

The above phrase will remain indelibly engraved in my mind to my dying day. When people say "the blood froze in their veins" I know exactly what they mean. It speaks volumes for my constitution that I did not drop dead right there from shock and humiliation.

The incident occurred while I was a guest at the home of Harold and Madeleine Park in Katonah, New York. Outside, the rain was falling in one of the worst downpours this earth has known since Noah built the Ark.

Madeleine Park, a sculptress who had secured my services from the Harry Conover Model Agency, had called for me earlier in the day, where I was living at the YMCA on New York's West 63rd Street. We had driven to her home in Westchester County, where I was looking forward to a pleasant stay and the prospect of several weeks of steady employment.

Madeleine's husband Harold, a prosperous gasoline distributor, greeted us upon our arrival, and I was shown the studio where I would be working. It was above the stable of Pepe le Moko, a roan gelding that I was hoping to ride. Then I was shown to my room.

Dinner was announced before I had time to unpack more than a few essentials. We had just started on the first course when Richmond, the butler, came in from the kitchen to say that I was wanted on the telephone. This puzzled me as I had not told anyone where I was going. As I was walking away from the table Mr. Park jokingly remarked, "You are probably wanted by the police."

Little did he suspect how right he was. I picked up the receiver. Without any preliminaries a man's gruff voice asked me how one got to Oaknoll, the Park residence. Since I did not know myself, Richmond volunteered the information.

"But who are you?" I asked, "And where are you calling from?"

He ignored the first part of my question, but told me that he was calling from the Katonah railroad depot.

"We'll be right up," he said, and hung up abruptly. I returned to the dining room much disturbed, and repeated the curious conversation. Before we were finished with the next course, we heard the sound of an approaching car coming up the hill.

I hurried to the front door to find out who the unknown callers were—while they came in through the back door. This gave them the impression that I wanted to escape. The three men looked at me standing in the front doorway with undue suspicion, flashed a badge, and announced: "We are from the FBI and have come with orders to apprehend you."

Through the remainder of the evening I was dazed and confused. Had the three men been kidnappers, no one would have stopped them, as none of us had the presence of mind to question their credentials. One thing I do remember is the immense kindness extended to me by the Park family and their staff.

Without doubt, my arrest by the FBI on February 16, 1942, was the lowest ebb in a life replete with many other low water marks.

Ellis Island

One of them accompanying me to insure my return, the FBI men permitted me to go upstairs to repack the bags that I had barely opened. Then, without further explanation, they pushed me into their car, and during the trip back to Manhattan the malevolent trio did not address one single word to me.

Our first stop was City Hall, where I was fingerprinted and had mug shots snapped of me, full face and profile, like the "wanted" posters that hang in every post office. Then I was delivered to Ellis Island by the three FBI men who had arrested me.

It was late at night when we arrived. I sat drenched to the skin while they examined and confiscated most of my luggage. The Vuitton and Cartier labels on the baggage seemed a source of annoyance to the examiners, and I could hear their derisive and abusive remarks.

Finally, I was handed a rough blanket and pushed into a small, dark room. The stench of unwashed bodies, tobacco, bad breath and stale air hit me like a bludgeon. Feeling my way in the darkness, I found an empty cot and lay down without undressing. Despite the unforgettable horror of the evening, I fell asleep at once from physical exhaustion.

Judging from the snores I was not alone, and the next day I found out that my cell companions were all seamen of different nationalities who had jumped ship rather than face an Atlantic crossing and the danger of being sunk by a German sub.

In the morning I was hauled from this cell and taken to an enormous room resembling a railroad station, where dozens of men were milling around. I later learned that the women were kept separated from the men, even if the detainees were husband and wife.

The first of all the many men whom I encountered was movie star Tullio Carminati. He was Italian and had made a huge success with Grace Moore in "One Night of Love." I knew him slightly. He was just emerging from the washroom with a paper cup in his hand, in which he was daintily stirring some Nescafé.

"Oh here you are at last," he said. "We have all been waiting for you."

"Who has been waiting for me?"

"But all of us, my dear fellow. The Axis members in New York."

As I was soon to find out he meant Prince Boni Boncompagni, opera singer Ezio Pinza, Count Lanfranco Rassponi, Prince Girolimo Rospigliosi, the Marchese Cesare Grimaldi, and other Italians, Germans, Austrians, Hungarians, and even some Frenchmen.

While Carminati was standing there chatting away in his worldly manner, a tall man went by with a chess board under his arm.

"Do you know each other?" Carminati asked. We both said no. "Prince Franz Hohenlohe, Prince Edmondo Ruspoli."

"Do you play chess?" Ruspoli asked. I said I didn't.
"Then come with me. I'll teach you." We sat down
on one of the double-decker bunks—there were no
chairs—and he proceeded to give me my first lesson.
This is how my nine months at Ellis Island began.
The food was plentiful, and the view of downtown
Manhattan was breathtaking, although all of us would
have preferred having our breath taken by the view of
Ellis Island from Manhattan. Twice a day we were
allowed out for a constitutional. There was a guard at
every door, and we were constantly being counted.

It must be admitted that some of the guards behaved
more like friends, at least toward me. I was arrested in
February, wearing heavy clothes, and when it became
hot, I had nothing but my tweeds to put on. One day, as
I was passing in front of him, one of the guards, looking
embarrassed, shoved a parcel into my hand.

"For you", he said, "from my old lady."

"For me? From your wife? But how does she even
know I exist?"

"I've told her about you. She thinks it's a shame
you being here, so young, and in such hot clothes."

The parcel contained all sorts of light summer
clothes, tee shirts and more.

We were allowed to receive mail and packages. But
of course everything was censored beforehand. Visits
were allowed once a week. Madeleine Park, in whose
house I had been arrested, came on every visiting day
through snow, slush, rain, and heat. I certainly wasn't
worthy of so much kindness.

All of us at Ellis Island were waiting for a hearing which would be established whether we would be interned or released. Mil, the only one of my family who was still free, never came to see me. She judged that her daughter, interned in Pennsylvania needed her more. She was right. I never tried to take my life, whereas Steph did try it. My hearing came in summer and it was judged that I was too dangerous to be let out. I was sent to my first of three internment camps.

Internment

The Roosevelt administration having decided that I was too dangerous an alien to be released from Ellis Island, I was sent to Camp Meade, and given the choice of being interned with Germans or Italians. I chose the Italians, figuring that this would give me an opportunity to learn their language.

The Italians and I left Manhattan in a sealed-off train, all windows heavily shuttered. Camp Meade was run by the U.S. Army, and we were there only briefly before being moved to Camp McAlister in Oklahoma. It was a bleak spot, surrounded by barbed wire and little more. But the Italians have a way of turning wherever they are into a bit of Italy. We soon had two football teams, and a marvelous set of cooks: one was the Marchese Cesare Grimaldi, the second was Prince Girolimo Ruspigliosi, and the third was an ex-con with a broken nose and a heart of gold. The ex-con, whose name I forget, was a specialist in making pies. At some point he decided that I was an object worthy of pity. The pies he baked to compensate for this sad state of affairs were put under my bed covers, still hot and redolent of apples, boysenberries, or whatever other preserves he could lay his hands on.

"Go look under the covers of your bed, kid," he would whisper in passing, out of the corner of his mouth. In return for these acts of culinary kindness I would buy him shaving lotion by the gallon at the PX, which he drank mixed with an even more lethal liquid that he made out of fermented potatoes. Then he would stagger back to the kitchen and bake me more pies.

By the end of my "term" in Oklahoma, where I learned Italian exactly as I had intended, I was shifted for the third and last time—to Camp Kenedy in Texas.

Mission to Saint Elizabeth's

It was wintry and snowing outside Camp Kenedy in Texas, but in the kitchen where I was doing KP duty, the steaming heat was suffocating. Wearing pants and a rubber apron with no shirt, sweat poured down my face and blood poured from my fingers where I had, for the umpteenth time, cut myself in the soapy water on one of the big, heavy-duty meat choppers I was washing.

We had KP duty at the internment camp on a rotation basis, but many internees were wealthy Germans—mostly big plantation owners who lived for many years away from their native Germany in such South and Central American countries as Guatemala, Honduras and Ecuador. They had become completely unused to doing any menial, physical tasks which we take more or less for granted elsewhere.

These people were ardent Nazis. Seen from afar, from their *fincas* and *estancias*, the new Hitler regime seemed attractive to them. They had left an impoverished Germany in the 1920's and had envisioned themselves one day returning to their homeland in triumph, with money earned raising sugar cane and bananas. Like themselves, that homeland had now become prosperous, "thanks" to one Adolf Hitler.

Latin America had no internment camps of its own, so under a little-known agreement between the United

States and most of the Latin American Republics, these avowed Nazis had been rounded up and shipped to various U.S. camps. Among them was the one in which I was incarcerated.

When it came time for KP duties, the Nazis would not soil their hands. They relied on others who were willing to work against a dollars and cents remuneration. This was not actually cash, as all our money had been taken from us. Instead, there was a system of coupons with which we could purchase bare necessities such as soap, toothpaste and a few Hershey's bars at the camp's PX.

The money we earned volunteering to work in place of others was entered on a ledger, to be paid out to us in the distant future upon our release. Meanwhile, we could do our PX shopping. When I was finally released after more than two years of internment, I had accumulated quite a sizeable amount.

There were several thousand internees at Camp Kenedy, so KP was a day-long duty. As soon as you had finished washing the breakfast dishes, you started on the ones from lunch—followed by the plates, pans and pots from dinner.

One afternoon, a guard came over to me. We were familiar with all of them and had a nice relationship totally unaffected by the poison being distilled daily in the columns of Walter Winchell, Robert Ruark and others.

"Franzi", he said, "Drop what you're doing and come with me. The old man wants to see you." The old man was Mr. Smith, the head of our camp, and a most humane man.

"Come right in, Franzi", he said, when I appeared out of the snow, bare-topped save for my kitchen apron, perspiration still dripping from my face. As I sat down, he placed a jacket of his over my shoulders, probably averting a case of double pneumonia.

"You've heard about your grandmother?" he started.

I had, of course. We all had, for there were radios in the camp and the juicy story of an enemy alien with a most un-American name being arrested in the streets of Dallas, Texas (where she was obviously up to no good and spying for Hitler), by the FBI, had been on all the front pages and on every radio news program across the country.

That she was a helpless old woman in her seventies, who spoke bad English, was terribly short of money because all she possessed was "frozen" in a bank in England, who lived modestly in a small hotel and minded her own business, and who was totally apolitical and hated Hitler, was not mentioned. Her picture was not shown in any of the papers; had it been, many fair-minded Americans would surely have deluged the papers and the Justice Department with protests.

Mil had been thrown into an insane asylum in Dallas, released, left Texas for Washington, re-arrested and thrown into another insane asylum.

"You know," said Smith, as he turned his back to me and went to stand by the window, "I am ashamed. I am deeply ashamed of what has happened and is still happening. I love your grandmother. The few times she has been here to visit you . . . I have grown very fond of her. She is a good woman, an intelligent woman, one of nature's great ladies. What is happening to her is shameful and must be stopped! There are others in our government who think as I do. Something must be done and you must help us."

At this point, I almost burst out laughing. "You want *me* to help *you* get my grandmother out of the asylum? I don't know if you've noticed, but I'm your prisoner and live behind three rows of barbed wire! Besides, who are these people who feel as you do?"

"I was afraid you'd ask me that. I cannot tell you, except that they do exist. You are bitter now, after all that has happened to you and your family. But you still have friends. You've not been completely abandoned. Believe me. Trust me. There are still people in Washington who are decent. We do not want you to be able to say you have been treated with such flagrant injustice once this was over. Yours is a prominent family and what we, as a nation, have done to you will spread around. We want to avoid that."

"What do you suggest?" I asked.

"First of all, I shall release you." At that, I almost jumped out of my chair to embrace him.

He smiled and put up one hand. "I'll release you on parole. But there are many buts. To begin with, of course, I can't let you go gallivanting around the country alone. I'll give you one of the guards to accompany you. And you must use a bogus name. If the papers get hold of the fact that the son of the "dangerous" Princess Stephanie (he had the grace to smile at this) is on the loose, there will be hell to pay and I'll lose my job."

"But where will I go? What will I do for money?"

"Not so fast. I'm coming to that. You will go straight to Washington. As for money, don't worry. The government will foot the bill. The guard will be provided with sufficient funds and pay everything for you."

"What will I do once I get to Washington?"

"You'll be on your own. You must use your wits. But, by hook or by crook, you must get your grandmother out of that asylum where she does not belong. Lie, say anything you please, but *get her out!*"

"And what do I do with her then?"

"That's the $64 question. You must find a quiet spot where she can live for the rest of the war without the danger of being grabbed a third time. No big city like Dallas or Washington. Someplace preferably in the country. When you've settled her in, you return here."

"Can I discuss this with my mother?"

"Yes, you may. I'll put in a call to her right now." My mother was then in a former women's prison just outside Dallas. She had been there, a prisoner of the United States Immigration Service, since shortly after Pearl Harbor. The conversation was monitored, of course, but still it was wonderful to hear her voice after so many years.

When I started to tell her the incredible, wonderful news, Steph cut in impatiently, "Yes, yes, I know. They've told me. But what will we do to pay for Mil's expenses if you succeed in getting her out? She has to be able to live until the end of the war; and Lord knows when that will end."

I had no answer for that. But, as so often in conversations one has with Steph, she immediately answered her own questions.

"Let me think about it for 24 hours. I'll call you back tomorrow. I'm sure Foxy will permit me to do so." And she hung up.

Dr. Fox, head of that former women's prison, was not only a very remarkable woman, she was also eminently fair. It had not taken her long to realize that here, in Stéphanie Hohenlohe, was a flagrant miscarriage of justice. She saw that the other women interned there were dyed-in-the-wool Nazis, extremely hostile to Steph. They ostracized her, cut up her clothes, spilled ink on her bed, and made life miserable for her in other tormenting ways.

"One more thing," said Mr. Smith before I left his office to return to my pots and pans, "Don't mention this to any of your fellow inmates. No one must know."

The next day Steph rang back at the appointed hour. Smith and I were waiting in his office. True to her direct nature, she came straight to the point.

"You know that when I was arrested in Philadelphia, I was coming out of a cinema. I had dined at the Berkeley with Mil and was wearing a few pieces of jewelry. These are all here with me; Foxy has them locked up in her safe. If you tell me what train you'll be on, the day and, above all, your parlor car number, I shall try to get them to you. What you do with them after that will be up to you. But please, try *not* to sell them. Pawn them only so that I can reclaim them after the war."

While Steph had never hesitated to accept jewelry from admirers, from my father on, she had bought the bulk of them herself, at the price of toil and tears only she knew about. I promised to ring her back the next day with the information.

The night of my departure I was smuggled from my cabin by a guard. He was so silent that my three sleeping companions never heard a sound. I was given civilian clothes and, after receiving some final instructions, I and my guard, whom I shall call "Tex," left by car for the San Antonio railway terminal. There we boarded a train in great luxury. We had a drawing room to ourselves—not because of any generosity from the U.S. government, but because it was the safest way to prevent me from being recognized.

When we arrived at the whistle stop where Steph was to meet me, there she was: flanked by a prison matron and by Dr. Fox, herself. Although Steph had aged a little, she was very chic in a trim, tailor-made suit, and fragrant of "Femme" by Marcel Rochas. There was just time for a quick embrace, then Steph stuck one of her little lace handkerchiefs in my hand. In it she had wrapped a 30-carat diamond ring and a large clip from Cartier, whose central stone was one of the bluest in the history of modern-day jewelry. I shoved both into my pocket and we were off.

My odyssey had started. Frank Hill (my assigned pseudonym) was on his way to Washington.

When evening came, the train steward knocked on our door and asked if he could make the beds. I stepped outside to give him more room while Tex stayed in the compartment, chatting with the friendly black man. After I returned to the compartment, Tex asked me, "Do you know that porter?" I didn't. "Because he knows you. He knows you're no Frank Hill. He was on a train you traveled on before and remembers you gave him a good tip. And he saw your picture in the papers recently."

The best laid plans of mice and men, etc. . .

In the middle of the night, our train ran into another one. It was a slight enough accident that I, always a sound sleeper, never even woke up. Nevertheless, we were hours late reaching St. Louis, Missouri, where we were to change trains.

The station was crowded with civilians and servicemen jostling each other for every inch of space. Never out of his home state before, Tex set down our suitcases and said, "Stay here and look after the luggage. I'll go and see if I can hustle up some seats on another train."

"Oh, no, you don't! You're not going to leave me here all alone. What if I get picked up by the police, standing here with no identification and using a phony name? Who'd believe my story? And how do you know I won't run away? All your money is in that suitcase; you told me so last night. Anyone can cash a government voucher just by signing it."

He looked at me, shrugged his shoulders and walked away, leaving me standing on the platform with $2,000 of government money—for one full, highly nervous hour.

When Tex finally returned, the reason he had been gone so long became apparent. He'd cabled Washington about our delay, and had arranged for another drawing room. Having once tasted the life of luxury, he was not about to relinquish it.

At last we arrived at our destination, to be met by two FBI men at Union Station. They flashed their badges, verified who we were, and escorted us to a grade-B hotel near to the station. They would return for us at 10 the next morning.

So there we were, Tex and I. It was still early and the excitement of being "out" had worn off a little. The prospect of spending the whole evening with that pleasant but simple cowboy seemed flat.

"Tex," I said, "I want to ask you something."

"Shoot."

"You're an American, right?"

"Right."

"And I'm not. I'm Hungarian and my country and your country are at war."

"Yeah, I guess so."

"It boils down to this. Hungary has no ambassador here in Washington. (It never had but why bring this up?) So, since the outbreak of the war, my country's interests have been represented by a neutral country, Sweden."

"Yep, I know," said Tex. "Those Swedish guys, Colonel de Laval and the other guy, come up to visit the camp twice a year."

"Exactly. That's what I'm leading up to. May I call the other guy? His name is Count Wachtmeister. After all, something might happen to me like being run over on our way to dinner. Will you let me call?"

I breathed a sigh of relief as he agreed. I looked up the number of the Swedish Embassy and was able, even though it was after office hours, to get Count Frederic Wachtmeister. This busy diplomat recognized my voice and very astutely understood at once when I said, "This is Frank Hill speaking."

Where are you, Frank Hill?" he wanted to know. And when I told him, he continued, "Think you'd be allowed to have dinner with me and my wife if I came by to pick you up?"

Tex and I went downstairs to meet the Wacht-meisters and, possibly influenced by the CD on the car and the general air of sophistication, Tex allowed me to be taken out to dinner.

We had a marvelous evening at La Salle du Bois, then the "in" place in Washington, and decided to take in a movie. Wouldn't you know that, with all the movies to choose from since I had not seen one in almost three years, we chose one that depicted a break from a concentration camp. As we sat doubled up with laughter, Freddy kept urging me, "Keep your eyes open and try to learn something. This may be the best way out."

Next morning, the two FBI men came for Tex and me and drove us to Saint Elizabeth's. While they all stayed in the car, I entered alone.

It was very cold; there was snow on the ground and the gray stone building with its heavily-barred windows looked anything but inviting.

I walked up to the receptionist's window, stated my name was Frank Hill, and that one of the patients was a family friend. The name was Szepessy. Could I please see her? Without any trouble, I was ushered to a barren waiting room. She would be brought to me.

There were wooden benches around the walls. The windows were barred just like a prison; the floor and walls were tiled. It was bitterly cold.

When the door was finally opened, I was not prepared for the pathetic figure who was shoved in. There, very small, frail, disoriented, and shivering with cold, was my grandmother. Her hair hung down in oily strands; she wore only a light nightgown and thin slippers. She was toothless.

As I ran to her and took her in my arms, she almost fainted from the shock of seeing me.

"You—my beloved boy! How did you get in here?"

"I can't tell you that now, Mil. The main thing is that I've come to take you away. But why are you dressed that way? Where are your dentures?"

"They have taken all my clothes away and my dentures because they claim they must mark them."

"But that is ridiculous!"

"I know," said Mil. "Everything is ridiculous."

"And where are your spectacles?"

"They took those away, too. They said I might cut my wrists with them. What day is it? What time? There are no clocks or calendars in here and I have lost track of time."

"Didn't you get my letters? My telegrams" My packages?"

She had not; Mil didn't even know if we were aware she had been taken to Washington. I'd sent her a bed-jacket that I had purchased from a mail-order house with money earned working at the camp. She had received nothing.

"You will never get me out of here, mark my word. You do not know what it's like in here. I can't describe it to you."

Mil's nose was running; she had a terrible cold. They would not give her a handkerchief, a Kleenex, or a comb to run through her hair.

"You are so thin, Mil. I've never seen you like this. You have lost pounds. Don't they give you enough to eat?"

"Yes, they do. But the stuff they feed us is so terrible I couldn't eat if I wanted to. I have no teeth. So I just take a little gruel and sit on the bed all day to keep warm. I can't read with no glasses; they wouldn't allow us papers anyway."

I was so upset, I couldn't take any more. Turning away to hide my tears, I said, "I must go now. I have much to do. But tomorrow I shall be back at the same time to see you and tell you more."

Back downstairs, I asked to see the head doctor. Surprisingly, this request was immediately granted. I was so full of fury I was ready to stick a knife into him. He turned out to be a she. Where I took the courage from I shall never know but when I got through, the walls were shaking.

One of the doctor's feeble arguments during our stormy session was that they were badly understaffed with no facilities for taking care of all the many patients under her jurisdiction. I countered that she was inhumanely neglectful and incompetent. Even if understaffed, surely there must have been someone to mark the belongings of Szepessy; she had been there a great number of weeks. The mail, she said, that Szepessy received was in German. No one on staff spoke this, so nothing had been done either with letters or packages.

I jumped at this opening. Since Saint Elizabeth's was quite obviously not in a position to look after its patients properly, why not release Ludmilla Szepessy to me? Being an old friend of the family, I was quite willing to look after her.

To my utter amazement, she accepted this proposition at once. That I was a young man hardly old enough to be anybody's "old friend" did not seem to occur to her. She said if I were willing to sign the necessary papers, this could be done relatively easily.

We had won!

Rescue from Saint Elizabeth's

When I returned the following morning, I found a much changed Mil awaiting me. Her hair was combed into a neat bun at the back of her head as she had always worn it. She had teeth in her mouth and glasses on her nose. Her cold was as bad as ever, but she now had handkerchiefs to deal with it. Mil still had no proper clothes, but at least she had been given one of her own warm flannel dressing gowns and was wearing stockings. I had brought her some things including newspapers and magazines so she could catch up on the outside world. Then I told her what my next step would be; to raise money for her to live on.

"Please be patient with me and trust me if I don't come back for a few days."

We—my guard, the FBI and I—spent many days running around Washington from one jeweler to another, one loan society to another, one pawn broker to another. All with no success.

The FBI gave up first; their gasoline was more precious than my safekeeping. Tex and I were on our own, but the poor fellow—a hardy cowboy in Texas—could not cope with our asphalt and concrete.

"Not so fast, Frankie," he would lament. "For God's sake, boy, I can't drag my arse another yard."

Stopping to rest at the Statler Hotel, I spied Noel

Coward heading straight toward me. I did not want to embarrass this dear old friend of the family, so I ducked behind a potted palm. I was not so lucky with Frank Redeker.

A worldly man, once divorced and later to marry an Egyptian princess, Frank's sharp eyes detected me and headed straight for me to shake hands. He'd known about my arrest and internment but he was quick on the uptake when I stuck out my hand and said, "My name is Frank Hill. How are you?"

"Of course, Frank Hill, I quite understand. And this is your traveling companion?" Saying this, he pointed his chin towards Tex, slumped, red-faced and footsore in one of the lobby chairs.

"Yes, and I'm not supposed to go anywhere without him."

Saying that perhaps we three could lunch together, he went over to Tex, introduced himself and invited us to lunch the next day. By this time Tex knew nothing untoward would happen if he left me alone for a few hours. Frank and I were able to lunch without his supervision.

I told Redeker my troubles about the jewelry and everything.

"Steph's jewels are too important for this hick town," said Frank. "Nobody dresses up, except the wives of Congressmen in costume jewelry at diplomatic receptions. You'll never get anywhere here in Washington. In fact, Cartier and Van Cleef are not even represented here. Your nearest bet is Philadelphia."

Tex and I explained my predicament to the Justice Department, and I was able to obtain permission to go to Philadelphia. Tex, however, was not to accompany me. It was almost Christmas and he was homesick for his family. Another guard took over. We bade each other an almost tearful farewell.

I was able to wring another concession from the Justice Department: I was able to contact Harold and Madeleine Park. They immediately said they would motor down to Philadelphia, and would meet me next morning in the office of the director of the Immigration Department.

I shall never forget that reunion! There were hugs and tears and laughter as we fell into each other's arms. Also present was a Miss Hershey—a civil servant who had been very kind to Mil. The Parks had arrived loaded down with presents, and before giving them to me turned to the director and said, "Please feel free to open everything and cut the cake in two so that you will know we haven't hidden anything.

After all the preliminaries, we started off on our rounds in Philadelphia, but that city was as bad as Washington. Many wanted to take the pieces on consignment, but none was willing to put down a large amount of money to acquire them, even on loan.

We informed the director of our singular lack of success and requested permission for another destination: New York. A few telephone consultations later, permission was granted. The Parks were able to obtain another concession: I was to spend my time in

New York with them as it was almost Christmas, and they wanted me to spend it in a Christian way under their roof.

When the four of us reached New York—Madeleine, Harold, my guard and I—it was rather late and we decided to eat dinner in Greenwich Village before continuing on to Katonah. The mood was festive and, as we waited for our drinks, the guard excused himself to call headquarters. Upon his return, we knew something was wrong. His face had dropped ten inches.

Permission had been withdrawn. I was to be put on the last ferry for Ellis Island.

Dinner was a lot less cheerful after that. Swallowing the last demitasse, we headed for the Battery. Harold slipped some money into my empty wallet and Madeleine promised to come for me the next day to assist me with my Manhattan jewelry-pawning rounds. The guard carried my few pieces of luggage to the ferry, turned me over to the authorities, hugged me and left. We were never to meet again.

Aboard the almost empty ferry, I was made to sit in a small unused cabin on the upper deck, to turn up my collar and pull down the brim of my hat. The papers must not get wind of the fact that this notorious criminal was out.

On the island I was smuggled in via the basement to prevent more leaks. After all—I had been there before and everyone knew me! (It is hard now to believe the fear in which people in those days had of the mighty Zeus, Walter Winchell, and a few lesser Olympians. They were the "guardians" of American life and morality. I can still hear the loathsome "Rat tat tat ta. Good evening, Mr. and Mrs. America and all the ships at sea" as it staccatoed out every night over the airwaves.)

One of the guards would go ahead, and beckon if the coast was clear, and the other guard and I would proceed as far as the corner from where he had whistled. This was repeated all the way through the whole building and up to the top floor. There a large former office had been made ready for me. It was totally bare except for an iron bed and a chair. From the ceiling dangled an electric bulb; a radiator spluttered in one corner. I was so tired I would have dropped into bed at once, but I felt I needed a wash. The nearest loo, shower and basin were in the cellar. The cloak and dagger routine was repeated in reverse.

Breakfast was left on a tray at my door; the man who traveled a mile and a half to bring my stone cold meals never saw me. The guard brought it in. This nonsense went on the entire time I was on Ellis Island that second time.

Madeleine waited for me the next morning, but so much time was wasted on the silly hide-and-seek stuff that I was able to accomplish very little. Before I could raise a dime, it was Christmas and all the shops were closed. I spent Christmas Eve and Christmas Day alone in my room, eating cold meals and looking out the window. Mr. Black, the director at Ellis Island, came to see me a few times before he headed home to his family for Christmas.

"Please, Franzi, don't cause me any trouble. I'm sitting on a powder keg. If it gets out that you are here and that a certain clique among us in the government is doing this for you and Baroness Szepessy, my goose is cooked. Many other people will find themselves without jobs."

"I'm not giving you any trouble. What more do you want? I'm sitting here all alone over the holidays like a con in a maximum security cell."

"I know, kid. Life's handed you a raw deal. I'll try to make it up to you as best I can. What do you want from the outside? I'll send it to you."

I took advantage of this and asked for magazines, a pen, writing paper and envelopes. And chocolate marshmallows!

He was as good as his word. I got it all.

One afternoon, while my guard was dozing in his chair by the locked door, I looked out the window and saw two figures walking arm in arm on the prisoner's walk. I recognized one of them at once. He was the distinguished, white-haired Prince Boncompagni.

"Bonny, Bonny" I called, hoping that he and not the guard would hear me. He did and looked up.

"Ah mon pauvre gosse," he said in French, *"Tu es de nouveau ici?"* But before I could answer, the window guillotined down on me viciously, missing my fingers by a fraction of an inch. The guard had awakened and, stealthily sneaking up behind me, had decided to punish this terrible prisoner.

"None of that," he shouted. "I'm gonna report you."

This was too much! Here I was, in a room I did not want to be in, locked up on the most holy day of the Christian calendar, fed cold meals, unable to take a pee when I wanted, doing everything I was asked to do to protect "them" from the wrath of Walter Winchell. And *he* was going to report *me?*

"You go right ahead, you old son of a bitch!" I said. "And see where it gets you."

After the holidays were over, I was able to make a very advantageous arrangement with the Provident Loan Society. Enough money was paid out for me to be able to take care of Mil. At the same time, Steph's jewels were kept safe until she could reclaim them.

I'm happy to say this was the first thing she did after the war—although not both pieces at once.

With the money safe in my pocket, I hurried back to Washington and got Mil out of Saint Elizabeth's in no time flat. I took her back to our hotel where a guard (my last one ever!) and I had to share a room.

I took her clothes, which smelled strongly of hospital disinfectant, and dropped them down the incinerator. And while she luxuriated in her first real bath since her arrest, I went our and bought her a whole new wardrobe—two sizes smaller.

After this, I bought a drawing room ticket from Washington to San Francisco. I had made arrangements with Mrs. Owler Smith to meet us and drive us directly to her home in Woodside above Palo Alto, where Mil would be a paying guest until war's end. Mission accomplished, I would then return to Camp Kenedy.

"Where are we going to go?" asked Mil when I came back with her new clothes and the tickets.

"I'm taking you to Mimi Smith's and settle you down there before I return to Texas."

"Oh, no, you won't," she replied calmly. She was now quite recovered from her ordeal; her resilience was amazing! Adjusting her stockings and dabbing a little powder on her nose, she continued, "That Mimi Smith doesn't even play bridge! And she lives in the woods at the end of nowhere. How could I even get to a cinema in Palo Alto?"

My mouth fell open in astonishment and dismay. It had never occurred to me that Mil would not gratefully fall in with my plans, after all I had been through. I had forgotten that my gentle little grandmother could be as stubborn as a mule. A mule? A team of mules!

We argued for an hour but at the end she merely said, "Well, you can take me to Woodside if you like. But I assure you I will not stay."

We entrained that night for our journey West. After everything had been unpacked in our drawing rooms with its communicating door in between, Mil came in and said,

"I think I like yours better."

"But they are identical!"

"No, they are not. Yours has a nicer view."

"How can you speak of views on a moving train where everything changes constantly?"

"Well, the angle at which one sees things is nicer in your compartment."

I wasn't going to argue that point. After all, I reasoned, she has just been through hell. And she *is* my grandmother. And I do love her very much. The guard and I changed compartments with her and finally she was happy. Until Chicago that is. Waiting for our Super Chief in the railroad lobby, she suggested, "Why not stay here? They tell me Chicago is a very interesting city. And Steph knows all those people who own department stores here. (She meant Townsend Netcher, Marshall Field and others.) I think this would be much more interesting than the dull hole of a Woodside."

White with fury, I snapped, "We're going to Woodside and that is *final!*" And we did.

Arriving in San Francisco, Mil was polite to Mimi Smith but not more. I felt agonies of shame that this lovable woman who had done so much for us could be treated so cavalierly by my little wisp of a grandmother.

Things had to get better; they couldn't get worse.

Mil the stalwart

In the days that followed, I had ample opportunity to observe Mil's phenomenal resilience. I remembered, too, that one day in the 1930's, while in the office of her lawyer, Maitre Mathieu Muller, on the Avenue de l'Opera, she had suffered an acute gallbladder attack brought on by injudicious eating habits.

More than a lawyer, Maitre Muller was an old and trusted friend and adviser. Mil always held that "My masseuse should be Swedish, my father confessor preferably Jesuit but my lawyer must be Jewish." Maitre Muller was indeed Jewish and he knew exactly how to handle the situation. "Lie down here," he said, stretching Mil out full length on his old-fashioned leather couch. Then he called his office boy, scribbled something on a piece of paper and said, "Get this at once from the nearest pharmacy. Run!"

The boy quickly returned with a small cardboard box of herbal tea. Maitre Muller had his secretary brew this and made Mil drink it. The tea, bitter, sugarless and scalding hot, had an almost immediate effect on her. After a short while, she sat up and soon left his office to go home, under her own steam.

When she died almost twenty years later as a result of a traffic accident, an autopsy would reveal that her gall bladder had burst some twenty years before. What the astonished Beverly Hills doctor who performed the autopsy did not know was how it had healed by itself. All he saw was the scar.

But there in Mimi Owler Smith's house, where our situation was so difficult, Mil was a hellion! In the beginning, an inspector from the Silver Avenue Immigration Station in San Francisco was sent out daily to see if I had not broken my word and run away, and generally to keep an eye on the two desperados. We did not resent his inspections in the least. Quite the contrary. In that quiet house, stuck away in the woods behind Palo Alto, his daily visits were a diversion and the social highlight of our day. We also made shameless use of him in those gasless days to which he, as a government employee, was not subjected. The minute we'd see his car rounding the bend, we would be ready to make him take us to town to do the day's shopping.

After a while we were told he would no longer visit us daily. Only three times a week. There was a general outcry from all of us at the news. "How could the U.S. government be so irresponsible?" we wanted to know. Mil and Mimi put it more forcefully, "What if Franzi runs away? Then what?" To our chagrin, the decision remained. Next, my guard was recalled. This was not hard to take. Mr. Smith, from my internment camp, called almost daily to find out if Mil was settling in. I had to reply that she wasn't and felt frightfully guilty as I did so. She was being completely beastly and I didn't know what to do.

His answer was always the same, "Give her more time after all she's been through. I'll check with you again the day after tomorrow."

One day in late February, the news came over the telephone, totally unexpected to me. I had been paroled! As I looked at Mil, standing near me and listening to the conversation, I saw a look of total triumph and great satisfaction on her face. It suddenly struck me like lightning. She had been impossible on purpose! In her wisdom, far greater than mine, she had planned it that way. Had she been meek and docile, they would have sent me back to camp. But, by playing her cards, she had forced their hands. I was free—perhaps not yet free as air, but certainly more so than I had been.

My personal agony had lasted from February 16, 1942 until February 28, 1944. I had been given a mock hearing on July 13, 1942 in New York City, condemned to be interned, and sent to a military camp in Maryland, Camp Meade, on August 14, 1942. The following month I had been given the choice of whether to spend my remaining time with Germans or Italians. I opted for Italians, and owe my present knowledge of that language to that move. I was sent to Camp McAlester, Oklahoma, an immigration camp.

On May 20, 1943, I was transferred again, this time to Camp Kenedy in Texas. My trip to wrest Mil from the clutches of evil started from that location on December 16, 1943.

Now, after two years and 12 days, I was free again. Mil and I bade farewell to the Smith family, and entrained for Los Angeles where I was allowed to reside, provided that I report regularly to a downtown immigration office and later on to a civilian volunteer who would be responsible for me.

As our train sped south, I was certain that now, at last, my hour had come. With the manpower shortage, I would find a job and keep Mil and myself in comfort. Possibly even luxury.

Bowling and baking

My new-found liberty turned out to be strenuous. I gave up looking for a white collar job when I realized that my recent internment was such a heavy handicap that few employers would dream of hiring me. At first I turned to the type of work where no questions were asked about my antecedents: I became a pin boy in a bowling alley.

My hours were roughly from after dinner until the last client had left the alley. In those days, automatic pin setters had not yet been invented. The pin boy had to hop down from his perch after every set and put the pins back in place manually, then hop right back up on the perch and draw up his legs in order to avoid being hit by flying pins and bowling balls. This simple act was actually quite painful, and by the end of a long night of setting up pins my back felt as if it would break in two.

To Mil, who was curious to know why I went out every night and stayed out so late, I did not tell the truth. I was afraid she would not understand it and make me stop, which would not have helped our finances.

From the bowling alley on La Brea Boulevard in west Los Angeles, I turned to baking bread at the International Bakery. This giant industrial bakery makes

"Wonder Bread," and one of my feeble jokes was that "It's a wonder they make it, with me as a baker."

There, too, the hours were long—but the work itself was not strenuous. I very often chose to do overtime, at pay-and-a-half. Walking to work in the mornings, often at 5 a.m., through the fragrant gardens of a Beverly Hills still shrouded in sleep, was a real joy.

It then came about that the United States armed forces, where I had volunteered to serve after being released from my last internment, and who had turned me down, decided to reverse their attitude, and out of the blue one day I received "the President's greetings"— that letter so feared by most young Americans of that period. To me it meant the exact opposite: acceptance, and the normalization of a pretty shaken-up life.

My decision to serve Uncle Sam was not one that I made rashly. I thought about it a great deal, and there was much weighing against it. How could I serve a government, a nation, that had treated me so badly, that had wasted years of my life, and where my own mother was *still* sitting imprisoned (she was the last woman prisoner in all of America to be released, weeks after the cessation of hostilities). All this was perfectly clear in my mind. But I also said to myself that I'd be asked in years to come, "And what did *you* do during the war? You sat it out in America and kept your arse good and dry, didn't you, while better men than you offered their lives?"

When I thought of this, enlisting seemed much preferable, and I have never regretted it.

A sad Christmas

Like every G.I. before he is about to be shipped overseas, I spent eleven weeks in basic training. My basic training took place at Camp Roberts, exactly half way between Los Angeles and San Francisco. Two hundred fifty miles each way.

Camp Roberts was gigantic. It was built on land obtained from the domain of William Randolph Hearst, whose castle San Simeon lay nearby.

When Christmas rolled around, the army allowed each man a few days' furlough, and those whose families lived close enough made ready to head for home. In my own case my family had been reduced to a father several thousand miles away in Budapest, whose house was being at that very time bombarded by allied planes, a mother interned for the duration (and a little more as it turned out) in a former women's-prison-turned-internment-center, in Texas, an aunt who was receiving even more allied bombs on her head in Berlin, a cousin who was fighting in the Free Czech army, several hundred Hohenlohe relatives in (mostly) Germany, and a lone grandmother who was living on my army pay, or what I was able to send her, In Beverly Hills, California. The home I would be heading for on Christmas Eve was on South Roxbury Drive, a small but pleasant apartment on the wrong side of the tracks of that city.

Many of the fellows had their own cars at Camp Roberts. I did not. I had my thumb to travel on. But wartime America was one big, friendly family, and no G.I. thumbing a ride was ever left very long by the side of a road. Frequently people drove miles out of their way, on rationed petrol, to deposit a soldier in front of his very door. I knew, therefore, that I would have no trouble covering the two hundred fifty miles and reaching home in time for the Christmas Eve celebration with Mil.

But fate stepped in and took the shape of a singularly sadistic officer whom I happened to pass in mid afternoon.

"Soldier" he said, "police this area before you leave camp. And see to it that *all* of it is policed, and well policed. I don't want to see a single cigarette butt on this parade ground before you take off."

The parade ground on which this conversation took place was as big as a major football field. I set to work at once, and, getting down on my hands and knees, with large rubbish bags to assist me, I began picking up cigarette stubs, dried chewing gum and match sticks. I did not stop until it was dark. The sadist officer had by that time long since disappeared. I made a beeline for the showers, threw on my winter uniform, for it was icy cold, and ran for the gate. And there I posted myself on Highway One, the long, long road which crosses all the United States from the Mexican border all the way to Canada, and which crossed Camp Roberts in its middle. It was pitch black and very few cars were driving by. At last someone gave me a lift, but only as far as San Luis Obispo, where I was deposited by the side of the road. I must have waited until well past 8 p.m. No one else drove by to give me a lift. At last I gave up, and somehow got back to Camp Roberts. Christmas had come and Christmas had gone. I crawled back into my cot in the empty barracks and fell asleep.

The noodle

My captain and I were sitting at a table over a meal. It was, of course, very seldom that an officer of the American army, democratic though it was, would break bread with a simple enlisted man, not even yet a corporal. But something between us had clicked, and so we sometimes sat together in some greasy spoon having a meal.

"Why" I wanted to know, "must an officer always be at the head of his troops? Would it not be just as easy and even better to observe the progress of the troops from the back?"

For an answer my captain took a spaghetti which was lying in a dish in front of us and placed it, nice and straight, on the linoleum of the table. He then took it between two fingers and pulled it along the table surface.

"See how nicely it follows my fingers?"

He then put his fingers in back of the spaghetti and tried to push it, which was, quite naturally, totally impossible. The spaghetti bent every which way.

"Does that answer your question?" he said.

Batangas

My first two army jobs overseas involved trucks. First I was assigned to roam the jungle paths of Batangas, on an army truck, delivering to and picking up from improvised, native laundresses, my buddies' fatigues, socks, skivvies, and jockstraps. All this laundry, redolent of men at war perspiring under the tropical sun, was easy enough to deposit to the laundresses, but far more difficult to pick up a few days later, as one jungle path bordered by palm trees looked pretty much like another to me. The laundry was washed in streams of yellow water and came back to us smelling dreadful, far worse than before.

I myself owned two uniforms: one clean, one dirty. Until, that is, a kindly officer by the name of Rodman de Heeren, who had known me as a toddler in Biarritz, gave me his castoffs, bless his soul.

After my transfer from the jungles of Batangas to a bombed out department store in the heart of Manila on the Escolta street, I was given another job, also involving an army truck. I plied back and forth between our censorship office and the bomb damaged post office in the center of the city, carrying sacks of mail. The difficulty in that assignment was the fact that in Manila, bombed out as it was, the shortest road from A to B was almost never a straight line. To avoid enormous craters in the middle of the roads I had to drive from A to Z to E to K to B. The bomb craters were enormous.

After several months in Manila I was skin and bones. If memory serves, I think I lost twenty pounds while stationed in the Philippines. I also escaped court martial by the skin of my teeth. My unit and I had been pulled out of Manila quite suddenly, and dumped in a camp awaiting orders. No one told us what this was all about, and why we were there, although the scuttlebutt was rife with rumors. The one thing we did know, however, was that we were strictly forbidden to leave camp under any pretext. So I slipped out and left camp under no pretence. I headed to the house of my friends Brailowsky, where I shed my sticky uniform, slipped on a pair of borrowed shorts and sandals, and sat down with them to dinner.

It was fairly late when we saw the headlights of an approaching jeep. It was my Hungarian buddy and compatriot, George Lehner, in great agitation.

"Quick" he shouted. "Jump in. They're looking for you all over camp. We're pulling out right now." And so we were. We boarded an LST, pulled out of the Bay of Batangas and ran right into a hurricane. Once that unpleasantness was over we continued on to Japan. The atomic bomb had exploded, the war was over. And occupation duty was about to begin.

Marie Pilar

The Spanish Marquise de Bethulia, whose Christian name was Marie-Pilar, was divorced, not very rich, and had three sons about my age, with whom I crawled about on the floors and under the furniture, in highly intellectual games, in our villa in Biarritz. Marie-Pilar was lucky and married a second time. Her husband, also a friend of my family's, was a very nice young Russian, Vadim Brailowsky. Before World War II broke out they moved to the Philippines and settled in Manila.

I, in American uniform, landed in Manila at the end of the war. There I learned of all the atrocities at the hands of the Japanese army that the Brailowskys had had to live through. But now they lived again in a very nice house in the country club district, and that house became my home away from home whenever my army duties allowed me to take an hour or two off. One might have expected Marie-Pilar, who had been interned in the notorious prison of Santo Tomas, to have lowered her rigid Spanish standards somewhat. But such was not the case. Her greatest gripe, to use an army term, was about her servants, who, according to her, just weren't up to scratch as they had been before, and never slipped out of their sandals, as they were supposed to do, Philippino style, before entering her sitting room! Of such hardships were Marie-Pilar's end-of-the-war days made!

The pom-pom girls

We seldom saw the face of a pom-pom girl, because our visits to their quarters almost always took place at night, and because they were invariably lying down, face upwards it is true, but in a dark type of stall in an unlit Philipino hut, usually round, which we reached by climbing up a steep ladder, as all the rural huts and houses were built on stilts. If you saw a pair of sandal-less small feet sticking our of the stall you entered it, if on the other hand you saw a pair of large G.I. boots, pointing downwards, you stepped over it and headed for the next stall.

The huts were pitch black. They had no light whatsoever. They were also completely devoid of water, running or otherwise. A few pieces of Kleenex of dubious cleanliness took the place of water. All we knew about these pom-pom girls was that they were young, very, very young, for the war and the poverty of the Philippine Islands made it imperative that the daughters of a household should go out and earn a living at a tender age. Not only did they earn their own daily bread, and by that I mean bowl of rice, but quite often that of the entire family.

We expected the pom-pom girls to be riddled by every venereal disease found in the books, but that didn't worry us because on returning to our camps we were obliged to pass through a large medical tent where corpsmen and doctors awaited you. The first order was "Let down your pants." Then came "Pull out your pecker and stand over this basin".

The corpsman then approached you with a large syringe, big enough to make strong soldiers tremble. In this was a big dose of red permanganate. This was injected into your you-know-what, and the corpsman or sometimes doctor, then barked his last but one order: "Hold it until I tell you to let go."

When the let go order came, it seemed to us that our life blood was running out of us, between our legs, into the metal basin. But venereal diseases we never got, not in my unit anyway.

And so we returned to our cots, after a romatic evening under a tropical sky.

Japan

Japan and I hit it off from the first moment of my landing, as I handed some candy bars to a gaggle of kids who were standing on the deck of Yokohama when my LST landed there soon after Hiroshima. To my delight they ate the candy rapturously instead of looking at me as though I were trying to poison them. This, I decided, was a good sign for all my future relations with Nippon.

Unlike other G.I.'s who knew no one in this far-off country, I arrived with a good supply of letters of introduction from friends in the States and in Europe who had been in the Far East before the war. There were also some Japanese school friends who gave me a link to the Imperial family.

The American army, as in Manila, opened the prisons and the internment centers, and herded all the non-Axis diplomats into one single Hotel, the Maranuochi, pending their repatriation to their different homelands. Among these was a young Italian University professor, Fosco Maraini, whose wife was a Sicilian noblewoman, the Duchess of Salaparuta—Topsy, for short—and a former Hungarian-born flirt of Pop's, the Comtesse Tascher de la Pagerie. Her husband was an attaché at the French Embassy, and Illy Tascher went on, a few years later, and with another husband, to become French ambassadress in Ankara.

All these people opened their arms wide to me. I was their breath of fresh air after years of prison life. It soon became apparent to me that I would have to do something for them in return. But what? Had this not been post-war Tokyo I would have opted for giving a dinner party. But a dinner party in a city where there was no food and consequently no restaurants?

Inspiration came to my rescue. On one of my early weekends away from Tokyo I had met three Japanese University students. One of these, Count Takio Kato,

Corporals George Lehner and Franz Hohenlohe,
the Rascals of the Regiment.

was the son of divorced parents. His father, Count Kato
Sr., had given his wife by way of alimony . . . a geisha
house. And Countess Kato ran it very efficiently. I
thought that surely a geisha house must be able to get
around the sticky problem of lack of food! I approached
Takio on the subject. Would his mother let me give a
dinner party in her geisha establishment, "The House
on the Good River"? And would she be able to find
enough food for about a dozen people? Takio came back
with the answers to my two questions: yes, she would,
and yes, she could. So the first hurdle was cleared. The
second one was that no lady, at least before the war,
ever set foot into a geisha house. I started with Illy,
who was a bit of a free spirit, and invited her first.
Would she consent to come to a dinner party in a
geisha house? I knew this was not done, but the
circumstances were such that I could hold my dinner
nowhere else. Of course she would come, was her
answer. Wild horses could not keep her away. Next
came the Italian ambassadress, Signora Indelli. She
almost jumped with joy at the idea. And so it went.
Even beautiful, tall Sunuko Inouye, the number one
concert pianist in Japan, who, having studied in Vienna,
spoke German as well as I, accepted. She, however, had
a problem of transportation as she lived in a fashionable
but remote quarter of Tokyo, and had no gas for her car.
I told her I would dispatch two of my friends, Sergeant
Davis and Corporal Lehner, who were also guests, to
pick her up in one of the motor pool jeeps.

As I later learned, the two boys set out but to their

Lovely Sunuko Inouye,
Japan's foremost
concert pianist.

discomfiture the motor pool was locked that night, which had never happened before. What should they do? The only solution was to pick up Sunuko by streetcar. And this they did. When they arrived at her lovely art deco villa, she was ready and waiting for them—dressed in a splendid brocade kimono with getas on her feet. She must have looked wonderful and I'm sorry I did not see her. When Davis and Lehner told her that they would have to proceed to my dinner by streetcar, she did not turn a hair. Bidding them sit down and offering them a drink, she went back upstairs. To travel in an elaborate kimono in a public streetcar, clambering up and down steps, would have been impossible. When she returned downstairs she had changed from head to foot and looked stunning. She was wearing wonderfully cut grey flannel slacks with a fluffy, white turtleneck sweater. And over the sweater mini tails in navy blue with gold buttons. She was smashing.

Because of the novelty and the excitement of the

evening all the geishas of "The House on the Good River" were kneeling around us, and no cup of sake was ever left empty for very long. Food was delicious, and my commanding officer kept everyone in stitches with army tales. The evening was a roaring success. But toward dessert I faced a moment of panic. There was a small stage at the end of the private room in which we were dining. Suddenly I saw the curtain part dramatically and a troupe of dancers began performing. Takio was sitting beside me, and I whispered in his ear.

"Am I going to have to pay for this on my twenty-one dollars a day once a month? Who ordered them?"

"Keep your cool" he replied, "They are performing for free. They have not been on a stage since before the war. They are the most famous troupe in all Japan, and when they heard you were giving this party they wanted to have the honor of being the first troupe of dancers to perform again. It is their present to you."

At that explanation I started breathing normally again, and if I'd been a drinking man, I would have had a cup of sake.

Apples Myakami

One of my first purchases in Japan was a pair of skis. I acquired them in Tokyo where the shops had virtually no merchandise, but remained gamely "open for business" all the same. One might find two pairs of high button boots at one counter, three opera glasses at another, an ivory back-scratcher at the next, and nothing else in the entire rest of the store. But all of it was displayed, sold, and wrapped with the most exquisite elegance. The skis were such an incongruity that I could not resist them. I came across them in a department store and walked back to barracks carrying them on my shoulder. It was September and the weather had not yet turned cold. The Hiroshima and Nagasaki bombs having exploded hardly a month before, nobody in his right mind was thinking of skiing. And to most of my fellow G.I.'s, Japan stood for the tropics. Why, I don't know. Tokyo is, after all, the same non-tropical latitude as Philadelphia! But no one had yet associated Japan with snow or the possibility of winter sports.

When I walked into the barracks carrying my new skis, I was greeted with guffaws of good-natured ribbing. The more so as the skis had no bindings! I later had to send to the States for these, where my sporting grandmother, Mil, came across nobly with a pair of Kandahars from California. That day, however, I was

Atop Mt. Fuji.

ragged and tackled and thrown up in the air and caught in a blanket until everyone was exhausted from laughter.

But when the weather turned cold (which it did much sooner than expected) and it started to snow, I was the only one equipped to take advantage of it! Later, the U.S. recreational services distributed sporting equipment which also included skis.

The war being over, we all had our weekends free from late Saturday afternoon until reveille Monday morning. So, with the first powder snow, and Saburo, my recently acquired Korean orderly (I, myself, being a PFC!) to carry my gear, I headed for the Japanese Alps. Seeing them for the first time, I was overwhelmed by their beauty. So much so that I did not have it in me to keep all this enchantment to myself. I told some of my friends, G.I.'s and WACS alike, what they were missing. Soon the more adventurous, or those who had done some skiing before, started to join me. None of us occupation troops had to pay our fares on trains. All transportation was free.

Whenever I traveled alone, Saburo would precede me to the station to apprise the station master of my imminent arrival. By the time I showed up a little later, instead of having to stand on drafty railway platforms, waiting for trains whose punctuality was still unreliable, I was received with smiles and endless bows and usually ushered into an office or small waiting room. Tea was brought in, a brazier placed at my feet, and the waiting made as comfortable as circumstances in a defeated postwar country permitted. Such was the power of the

U.S. uniform, perhaps slightly aided and abetted by my personal chutzpah.

When we traveled in large groups these niceties had to be dispensed with. But sometimes, when we were lucky, we had whole carriages to ourselves. One member of our clique was a lieutenant, a naturalized German Count. He was a railway buff and nothing would do but that he had to climb, while the train would hurtle full speed through the night, from our carriage into the locomotive cab. There he was received, admittedly, with some surprise but much deference, especially when he explained to the two locomotive drivers that he knew as much about the running of engines as they did. Pretty soon he was in control of the train, with one of us volunteering as stoker, while the Japanese crew sat by, smiling, and quite relaxed.

None of us ever left Tokyo without our full supply of K rations for the weekend. But we also carried chestnuts and apples which we took to roasting by the roaring fire of the locomotive. Our ski poles were used as roasting spits. These hot snacks were baptized apples Myakami, after the name of the tiny village that was usually our destination.

When Italian Professor Fosco Maraini, who was awaiting repatriation after years of internment in Japan, heard of our expeditions, he was saddened that his civilian status precluded him, a former ace skier, from joining the fun. I soon changed all that by lending him one of my uniforms and smuggling him into our G.I. group. At first he was very hesitant as he was still traumatically haunted by the memory of what he had been made to endure at the hands of his Japanese jailers. In Tokyo he seldom ventured into the street without looking over his shoulder to see if he was being followed. The Saturday on which I made Fosco join us was his last weekend in Japan before returning to Italy. He and his family were to board a boat in Yokohama on Monday morning. Topsy, his wife, knowing that once he felt snow under his feet he was as good as lost to her, issued a parting threat: "If you're not back in time and we miss the boat through your fault, I give you warning that I will divorce you!"

Years later she did so anyway.

When we reached Myakami, a hand painted poster announced a slalom race. Fosco read this and disappeared.

"Where have you been?" I asked him later.

"I tested the course."

"How was it?"

"Pretty rough."

But on Sunday morning Fosco was one of the entrants. And at the finish he was number three. Not bad for a university professor who had not stood on skis for fours years and languished, undernourished, in various Nipponese prisons.

But just as his wife, the dashing former Duchess of Salaparuta, had feared, now that he had tasted the exhilaration of skiing again and had done so well in the slalom race, there was no holding him back. Instead of catching the next train back to Tokyo, he lingered on with all of us, eating, drinking and singing raucous songs. At last, after the last caterpillar tractors had ceased operating between our village outpost and the railway station down in the valley, I threw him out, not wanting to have the Marainis' divorce on my conscience. It was pitch dark by then. The stars were twinkling and the night was clear. Still, to navigate several miles downhill on skis, at night, over unknown terrain, was foolhardy to say the least. Fosco thought otherwise. The innkeeper gave him a burning torch like those used in medieval times; and with that in one hand he made the downhill run in time for the last train.

Later, when I saw him again in Europe, after he had been on several Himalayan expeditions, and taught the young Dalai Lama to play football, he gave me an old pair of his mountain climbing boots. I can now truthfully say, "These boots have been to the top of Mount Everest."

I carefully avoid adding, however, that I was not wearing then at the time.

Soap

Every American G.I. who has done occupation duty is automatically suspected of having indulged in black market activities of one sort or another. In Japan, in addition to my meager "twenty-one dollars a day, once a month," I was making the equivalent of $2,000 monthly on the side, and all of it was on the up and up.

My Korean houseboy, Saburo, had been perfidiously snatched away from me by my commanding officer when I was soft-hearted and foolish enough to loan him out to "Do a spot of cleaning in GHQ."

In time I achieved the minor miracle—through the good offices of Baron Gregorio Cavalchini—of finding another Oriental pearl to replace him. This second boy was authentically Japanese and went by the name of Tako. But in-between there lay an arid stretch, a desolate period, where I had to shine my own boots, polish my brass buttons, iron my uniforms, and run my own errands. During this bleak interval I made the acquaintance of the laundries of Tokyo, to which I had to confide my washing, now that I had no private hireling to do if for me. I also discovered that they washed without soap! They did this by using lots of water, of which the islands of Nippon contain a plentiful quantity, much rubbing, and beating the clothes with merciless vigor against unyielding stones! The latter process is not designed to prolong the life span of any garment! But soap could not be found in all of Tokyo for love or money.

This gave me an idea. I have always been an early riser. As my buddies would often remark in daintily chosen words: "For Chrissakes, Franzi, can't you keep your arse in your bunk a little longer?"

But in spite of the cajoling words, I could usually be found in the showers or doing my daily calisthenics long before my comrades in arms had opened their sleepy little eyes.

To anyone not acquainted with the military life as led in Uncle Sam's army, I have to describe the size and proportions of such a "shower." Ours was installed on a floor above the rooms in which we slept. It had the approximate dimensions of a ballroom at the court of Marie Antoinette. All around the walls were spigots that dispensed unlimited quantities of hot and cold water. Such a luxury to me, raised in hot water and expense-wary Europe! There were also, of course, containers for soap. But most of the soldiers, untidy and wasteful as only the sons of a very wealthy nation can be, would seldom use these for the purpose to which they were intended. Instead, they would lather themselves with a bar of soap a few times, then drop it right in the middle of the shower room, to buy a new cake at the PX (for damned little money, courtesy of the U.S. taxpayer) on the very next occasion.

The result was that in the early mornings, before our Japanese cleaning crews showed up to clean and tidy for the day, the shower floors were littered with perfectly good pieces of soap from the previous night's ablutions. It was dangerous as hell to life and limb, as stepping on the slippery stuff you could break your ruddy neck.

"What can the cleaning crews in all these showers, on all these floors, in all these American barracks all over Tokyo possibly be doing with so much wastefully leftover soap?" I asked myself.

"Like the candle-stub removers of Louis XIV," I answered myself, "whose duty and prerogative it was to clean out all leftover candles from all the sconces, chandeliers and wall brackets at Versailles every morning, these guys will become millionaires in one generation! Did not their French predecessors marry off their daughters into the nobility before the Sun King had been carried to his grave?"

"What they can do I can do better" I further soliloquized, in the manner of Annie Oakley.

With Tako to assist me, I would get up early, usually between 5 and 6 in the morning, ascend to the various showers, and collect all the soap that was littering the floors. The quantities we collected proved to be quite overwhelming. It soon became a problem of knowing what to collect them in, and where to stow all this away.

The first problem I solved by going to see the cooks in our mess hall. "What do you guys do with your empty tin cans?" I asked. These containers were about the size of large beer barrels.

"We set them outside, and they get picked up by the garbage detail in the morning."

That was all I needed to know. Instead of the garbage detail, Tako and I started picking them up ourselves. Tako then cleaned them thoroughly from every trace of margarine, sugar or flour which they had contained, and they became our soap containers. After that, from Monday till Friday, we filled and stored them in Tako's "bedchamber"—the space behind the bookcases where Saburo had slept before him.

All this was easy as pie. The difficulty arose when it came time to get these suspicious-looking containers past the M.P.'s who stood guard at our barracks doors. There was nothing illegal about what I was doing; but I felt certain that my operation would have aroused their suspicions. Worse, it might

The soap flake money was converted into silk, brocades, ivory, lacquer —and pearls!

have given them ideas of emulating my example.

The soap was consequently smuggled out every week, with the complicity of some of my buddies, in their laundry trucks. Once outside the gates, I retrieved it at a pre-arranged point.

The best part of the game began at that stage. I made the rounds of all the laundries of Tokyo in my personnel carrier, offering my wares for sale. The first reaction of any laundry owner who had not dealt with me before was always the same: a suspicious and categorical refusal.

"No, no. Many thanks to honorable soldier. But me not want military police in shop."

When, however, they got to see my soap, and realized that what I was saying was true that they were merely leftover pieces, their resistance was soon broken and they became grateful customers. Out of my used bars of soap they made millions of soap flakes.

And I in turn converted this soap flake money into silk, brocades, pearls, ivory and lacquer, which back in the States became the dollars and cents on which I founded my return to civilian life.

Tobacco

After the successful launching of my career in soap, I branched out into other commercial ventures. It occurred to me that there was an equally shameful waste of tobacco. Most cigarettes were smoked no further than the halfway mark, then thrown away and a fresh one lit. Strewn around wherever G.I.'s gathered, the butts found their way into the incinerators.

This state of affairs had to stop. My houseboy, Tako, was again put to work, this time collecting cigarette butts in his spare moments. After all, I didn't have that many uniforms to press.

He and I would cut off all the singed edges—oh, shades of my Viennese childhood and the parsimonious kindergarten habits! We kept only the virgin tobacco. In Tokyo, cigarettes could be obtained by the local population from well-disposed G.I.'s at every street corner, so I sold my bags of mixed tobacco on my weekend forays into the rural hinterlands.

To say that I was greeted with open arms wherever I put in an appearance is putting it mildly. My progress always followed the same, well-rehearsed pattern. Tako and I would arrive at some village or small town and inquire for the name of the best Japanese-style inn. Western-type hotels I avoided. I could find better in the West itself.

This choice in itself made the locals look on my arrival with approval. Tako was then instructed to inform the innkeeper that I had merchandise to sell. This brought a courtesy call from the owner to my room. I displayed what I had: open sacks of tobacco. My host, judging that this was probably not loot, contraband or black market merchandise, smiled, bowed an inordinate number of times and withdrew. Within the hour my quarters would be teeming with villagers ready, willing and able to buy. As with the soap, this led to friendships which have lasted over the years.

I was dined and saki-ed in many delightful homes

that I would otherwise have never gotten to see and that my army buddies, spending their weekends on their cots, reading the funnies, never even imagined existed.

These agrarian populations, being less well-supplied with consumer goods than the more fortunate inhabitants of Tokyo and Yokohama, soon began asking if I could procure such precious items as shoelaces, hairpins, threads, needles, lipsticks, combs and buttons.

Even a wheeler-dealer such as I had no way to obtain all of these scarce commodities. But I soon enough found a way to remedy this. I would send a very small part of what I was earning from my soap and tobacco to Mil in California, with instructions to please betake herself to the nearest dime store to buy up large quantities of the desired goods and dispatch them to me. This she did with speed and relish, for her sporting instincts and sense of the ridiculous were highly developed. Her packages reached me like clockwork. Working in the censorship department, I had no difficulty clearing them through to my own desk.

With the money I earned selling "miscellaneous items," I bought more cultured pearls from Mikimoto, as well as jade, lacquer, brocade, silk and tortoise-shell.

Most of the Japanese had worked throughout the war in factories supplying the Imperial armed forces, and were flush with money. But the yen they had earned were of little use to them. Everyday articles, from toothbrushes to bicycle pumps, which they urgently needed, hadn't been manufactured for the duration and were consequently unobtainable. To me, however, these yen were precious. I could convert them into dollars and send them home to my U.S. bank. As for the pearls and brocades, these were the last things on earth the Japanese needed at that time. They were cheap and plentiful, and I stocked up on them for a rainy day.

More important than the material advantages were the human contacts I made, and the unique way all of this enabled me to get to know that wonderful country in depth.

One weekend, when the small village I'd chosen to visit proved to have no inn at all, I was standing rather disconsolately on the central square, surrounded as usual by a curious throng. Tako was off somewhere making inquiries as to the likelihood of finding quarters for the night, but I sensed that his quest would be futile. Then out of the crowd stepped a young Japanese man who spoke fluent German. He would, he said, be delighted to have me stay at his parent's home, if I would care to follow him. Of course I would. Night was approaching rapidly, and it was getting uncomfortably cold.

At his house I met his parents and sisters, to whose eternal credit it is that they showed no surprise at this intrusion. I gave them all my army rations, which they first wanted to refuse but finally accepted. We sat down to a delicious meal of fish and rice with a small portion of what I contributed. I'd learned to eat with chopsticks and no longer made too much of a spectacle of myself, sitting cross-legged on the floor.

The next day was Sunday, and they asked me what I wished to do. "If I were at home," I said, "I'd go to mass, for I am a Catholic."

They surprised me by replying, "So are we. There's a Catholic church in the village. Let's go." And we all went. When you have reached the point when you can kneel down in prayer with your former enemy, and pray to your common God, you know that you're at the core of what life is all about.

Bucky

When I was a student at Stanford University—after Oxford and prior to my arrest by the F.B.I.—I had a good friend from the Hawaiian Islands, Bucky Henshaw. He was an immensely popular boy, liked by everyone. After graduating from the university, Bucky went on to Annapolis, became an Ensign in the United States Navy, and was just in time to catch it full blast at Pearl Harbor. Bucky was made a prisoner of war on Wake Island, and carted off by the enemy to languish for the rest of the war in various Japanese prisons. Fortunately, thanks to the International Red Cross, his parents knew at all times in which prison their son was incarcerated.

Soon after my arrival in Yokohama, a large white hospital ship was just leaving, loaded with Allied stretcher cases. It was already under steam, ready to pull out of the harbor. Walking up to a sailor who was standing by his Morse lights on the quayside, I asked him if he could flash a message to the ship, inquiring if one Ensign Henshaw was aboard? The gob obliged. He blinked my question. Soon a message came back: Yes, he was. Bucky was one of the stretcher cases being shipped back to Honolulu. I told the signalman to let him know Franz Hohenlohe had just landed in Japan and that I would write.

Months later, when the International War Crimes

Trials began, I received a phone call in my office. It was Bucky, who had just arrived back in Tokyo. The Navy had given him the Lieutenant Commander rank he should have earned by then, had he not been captured. He was needed, along with some others, as a witness at the trials.

We spent a lot of time together. There was so much to talk about, to catch up with. On weekends he sometimes invited me to stay at the luxurious villa in the suburbs of Tokyo where he and the other witnesses—some French, some British—had been put up. I remember being very impressed with the splendor of the surroundings. Gurka guards patrolled the grounds, and the food was delicious.

One of the first things Bucky told me was that during the time of his long imprisonment he had

Bucky Henshaw (at right) with his family.
Bucky eventually became the producer
of a popular Hawaii-based television series.

converted to Catholicism. Since we were now of the same religion, I asked him to accompany me to Mass on Sunday morning. The church nearest to his quarters belonged to the Convent of the Sacred Heart. We went there together, and on the front steps ran into a friend of mine, the Japanese Marchioness of Hachisuka, whose little girl was then going to school with the Sisters of that Convent.

"What luck" she said "that I should run into you, Franzi. The Mother Superior has heard me speak of you so often that she would like to meet you. She is Bavarian and knows your family. We shall go and call on her after Mass."

And so we did. I introduced Bucky to the Marchioness, and the three of us sat together in a front pew. After the end of Mass we proceeded to the Mother Superior's little office behind the church. She turned out to be a delightful old lady, stout, jolly, and very cordial.

As we sat around her desk, chatting amiably, I noticed Bucky staring very intently at the Mother Superior. Finally, when a lull in the conversation gave him an opening, he said "Tell me, Mother, did you ever have occasion to come to a prison for Allied soldiers in the dead of winter?"

"Why yes, my son, I think I did on several occasions. Why?"

"Because, you see, I was born a Protestant. But during my long imprisonment I thought things over very carefully and decided to convert to Catholicism.

But I needed to know more about the new religion I wished to embrace. So I wrote a letter to Peter, Archbishop of Tokyo. What did I have to lose? He might answer me and he might not. But I figured that being a Catholic would outweigh his being Japanese. I was right. It did. He answered my letter and told me that the books I had hopefully requested would be sent to me. He was as good as his word. One day I was standing at my prison window, looking out. It was snowing heavily and bitter cold. My prison, high on a hill, was banked by snow. From a distance I could see a female figure slowly climbing the hill through the snowdrifts. As she came nearer I realized that she was a nun, and carrying a heavy parcel. After that she disappeared from my field of vision. But on the following day I was given the books I had requested, in English, which the Archbishop had the kindness to send me. But the nun, Mother Superior, that nun carrying those heavy books, I think was you?"

"Yes, my son, it was. And how happy it makes me to see you sitting her now that it is all over!"

Mama-San

Bucky Henshaw and I attended a rather grand Tokyo garden party, where Westerners and Orientals were mixing freely. There were many occupation officers in uniform, some ladies in their first post-war finery, a few Embassy civilians, newspaper correspondents of the Clare Luce caliber, and selected Japanese officials.

As we passed a certain Japanese gentleman who seemed completely at his ease and conversing amiably with everyone around him, Bucky became tense.

"What is it?" I was curious to know.

"That man over there" he replied, indicating Viscount Norizne Ikeda, the amiable gentleman we had just passed. "How much blood he has on his conscience! He won't attend many more garden parties after I am called to the witness stand!"

But Bucky's prison experiences were not all bad, and the best of them concerned Mama-San. A little old woman, she was the ever-cheerful wife of the porter in one of Bucky's jails. Despite the war, the adverse circumstances, the rationing, and the language barrier between them, Mama-San always came up with some hidden goodies for her boys, the Allied prisoners. Sometimes it was a bit of soap, sometimes a few cigarettes, some matches, or a candle stub to read by. All unimaginable treasures in those days of extreme hardship.

Many a time Mama-San was carted off by the Japanese secret police, and every time this happened the prisoners thought they would never see her again. But she always reappeared, often the worse for bruises and the obvious signs of having been beaten, but still smiling and uncomplaining. And never as long as they were there did she stop bringing them such small tokens to make their life more bearable. Bucky and the other prisoners swore that if ever they got out alive, they would return to Japan and give Mama-San a very, very special treat. Some died and never made it to that reunion. But Bucky survived with a handful of others, and the reunion with Mama-San took place during the time I was in Japan. Then years went by, and long after we had all returned to our respective homes I received a letter from Bucky which read in part:

"The last time I saw our beloved Mama-San was during a visit to Japan in 1964. By then her husband, the former prison janitor, had died and she was living in an old peoples' home in Sendai-north. I sent her money and she came to see me in Tokyo—third class on the train. When I asked her why she had come third class when I had sent her plenty of money to travel first, she said 'I always go third class. That's where my friends are.'

"We had a lovely reunion and during the following years I corresponded with her at least once each quarter. She, of course, responded in tidy little characters which were translated for me by a girl in Dad's office. Finally a letter came from the administrator of the Old People's

Home: 'Please do not send Mama-San any more money, Mr. Henshaw, as she is now very senile and does not use it wisely. Your last check for twenty-five dollars she cashed and spent the entire amount on candy. Then she sat on the lawn in front of our grade school and as the children passed her on their way home, each was given a sweet, until all was gone. I'm sure you agree with me that the money you send is for her personal welfare and not for such extravagances.'

"I replied: 'Dear Matron Furuya, the money I send Mama-San is for her happiness. If it gives her pleasure to spend it all on candy for school children, then that is what I want for her. Please permit her any indulgence as long as she lives. Believe me, she is deserving of this.'

"I never heard again from Matron Furuya. And Mama-San too, stopped writing. After a year I wrote a friend and asked that he call the home and find out about dear Mama-San. She had passed away quietly. They thought she was in her late eighties—but she would never tell anyone her age. Among her meager possessions was a small bank draft from me—which they returned. I cashed it and gave the money to our Filipino yard lady. She promised me she would spend it all on candy for poor children in her neighborhood.

"I'm sure that by now Mama-San must be a saint. I say 'by now' because these things seem to take so long to recognize. If we down here suffer from so much bureaucracy, think how dreadful it might be in Heaven where there are so many, many more people! Oh well— if she is not yet a saint—she is still an angel!"

Goodbye to the Army

When my time in the Army was up, and I was being made ready for my discharge, I was sent to a replacement depot—known to us G.I.'s as a repple depple—somewhere between Tokyo and Yokohama. The barracks we were in had been built pre-war by the Japanese military, and were in very bad shape. The roofs leaked all over whenever it rained, and it rained a great deal. We were a large number of guys all waiting to be shipped back Stateside, and our cots were so close together that you could not put your foot down between two of them. When it rained at night, we lay there in our wet misery, unable to move our cots an inch right or left to avoid the drizzle. I would cover up with my poncho as best I could, but to little avail.

Before many nights had passed, I had developed a goiter and could not utter a sound. What pain I suffered I shall skip over lightly. Every morning, as we stood lined up for reveille, an officer would call out our names. We were supposed to shout back, "Present!" but since no sound came out of my throat, I was given hell every day, on an empty stomach before breakfast, and every day by a different officer.

Finally the day of my departure dawned. I packed my bag, which was laden with loot I was bringing back from Japan. There was silk, lacquerware, brocades, cultured pearls, tortoise shell objects, and much more. It was, in a word, heavy as hell. I dragged it and myself up the gangplank of the ship that was to take me to San Francisco, feeling worse than ever before in my life. But halfway up to the deck I passed out. It's a wonder the bag and I didn't roll into the brink.

The next thing I knew as I opened my eyes, I was flat on my back in the ship's dispensary, with a doctor-officer looking down my throat. He shuddered at what he saw, and said, "Boy, you're in real bad shape! Why didn't you report your condition to the doctor at your replacement depot?"

Since I couldn't answer, I gestured for a pen and piece of paper on which I wrote, "I waited for this ship two years and didn't want to miss it!"

He laughed out loud and replied, "Sorry, buddy, but you are going to miss it. I can't let you travel in this condition. I'm sending you right back ashore to the Army hospital in Yokohama."

And so he did, to my consternation. There I was made to linger a week, until my condition was judged good enough to be put on a plane for the States. We landed at Wake Island, then Johnson Island—which is no more than a landing strip in the Pacific—then Honolulu, where I drank six milkshakes in a row at the airport, and finally, finally, Frisco!

I then spent a few more days in another repple depple, which I was allowed to leave on overnight passes. With one of these in my pocket, heading for an evening in town, I found myself sitting next to a sergeant

I did not know, who was in very high spirits. Rubbing his hands together, he turned to me and said, "Boy, oh boy! Does it feel good to be home! But I can't complain. I had a good war. Never got shot at, never lost an arm or leg, and never even caught a dose of the clap. But some guys had it rough. Why only the other day, would you believe it, here I was, standing at the railing of that Kaiser-built tub that brought me back from Yokohama, watching the guys come aboard one after the other. And one of them, poor cuss, could hardly drag his own arse up the plank, with a huge bag slung over his shoulder, when zowie! he passes out cold and they had to cart him off to the medics down below."

"Maybe so," I said, but that poor cuss is sitting right beside you!"

Of course, he didn't believe me. Miracles like that just don't happen.

* * *

After all that, you might think that I had done with the military. But I hadn't. there was another war in the offing, and some guys like myself are just made that way: they hear a bugle call, or a military march, and away they go. The war in the making was the Korean conflict, and before I knew it I again found myself in uniform—this time in the U.S. Navy. You can read all about that, if you feel like it, in my next book, *The Sailor Prince*.

Working for State

Back in civvies the old round of looking for a job started all over again. I found one with the State Department in Washington, D.C., followed by another at the United Nations. It was a very minor branch of the State Department: the Displaced Persons Commission. But saying "State Department" sounds better. Our offices in the old Rochambeau Building on Connecticut Avenue were shabby, but we were a merry bunch, and though the work we did was distinctly menial, we enjoyed our work and the lives that went with it.

The golden heart

During the year that I lived in Washington someone fell head-over-heels in love with me. I was delighted, flattered, and frightened because her love was so intense. Love letters accumulated by the gross, and also humorous little poems. For Christmas she gave me, among a quantity of other gifts, a dozen . . . jockstraps to wear under my swim trunks, each of which she had hand embroidered with a red "FH." This sounds quite ludicrous in cold print, but I was profoundly moved since I knew that such very intimate pieces of wearing apparel could not have been embroidered by her while sitting in the family circle. They had to have been stitched surreptitiously in the privacy of her bedroom, at night, encroaching on her normal hours of sleep.

But the most touching present of all was a small golden heart on which had been engraved "Mein Herz, Franzi, immer Dein".

Since I had no wish to invite inquisitive interrogation, I wore this "My heart, Franzi, forever yours" heart on a thin golden chain, tucked away in my trouser pocket where only I could see it. Also attached to the chain was a small golden pencil.

When summer came I left for a European vacation which took me, among other places, to Munich. While there, one of the Princesses of Bavaria asked me to spend the afternoon with her on Lake Starnberg where she lived. She received me—probably because it was more convenient for serving afternoon coffee—not in the drawing room, but in her dining room. In the course of the afternoon's visit the matter of a mutual friend's address came up, which I had but she did not.

"I shall give it to you" I said, and proceeded to pull the small chain with heart and pencil out of my pocket. But as I lifted it up the little heart detached itself and fell on the floor. We both saw it distinctly and I immediately dove under the dining table to retrieve it. Since we were, as I said, in a dining room, where there is practically no other furniture save a table and a few chairs, this should have been easy. No one could miss a glittering small object on a parquet floor! But it wasn't. The heart had vanished.

"Can you see it?" Princess Ruprecht inquired from above.

"No, not a sign of it."

"But that's impossible" she said and dove in right after me.

There we were, the two of us, the crème de la crème of European nobility, crawling about on all fours, like two dachshunds, under a dining room table, while our coffee was getting cold on top! But all to no avail. The heart could not be found. Finally we had to give up. I took this as an omen. Not a good one. And I glanced at my watch to note the time.

When I returned to Munich, by train, as I had come, I started walking from the station to my hotel, and on the way passed a small jeweler's shop. And there in the window lay a heart exactly like mine. Except for the engraving it could have been my heart so recently lost forever. I walked right in and bought it on the spot and immediately instructed it to be engraved "Mein Herz, Franzi, immer Dein." It was ready two days later. I have it still. But on my return to Washington an unexpected shock awaited me. My girl had taken the veil. She was in a convent. Her decision, as I found out from her family, had been taken on exactly the day and even the hour—taking into consideration the difference in time between Munich and Washington—when her original heart had disappeared forever.

Mae West

I met Mae West in the post war years in London where she had decided to take her play, "Diamond Lil," and was doing a standing room only business during its West End run. I saw it one night and thought it a brilliant piece of showmanship. There was a particularly effective scene where, sitting in profile before a dressing table in dim light, she showed herself totally nude from the waist up under a gossamer negligee which left nothing at all to the imagination. This was pretty heady stuff in the late 1940's. Even more startling was the realization that this formidable woman who even then was no spring chicken, should have such beautiful firm breasts which owed nothing to the corset maker's art. Clever as she was, she realized that even the prudish British law had nothing on her as long as she was covered. And covered she was in the most sexually provocative way.

After the play I went backstage to congratulate her, and told her, among other things, how well a certain spotlight had looked as it shone on her hair in a moonlight scene. She was most pleased to hear this because, she said, she wore a new wig in that particular scene, as an experiment, to see if its bluish tint would give the proper moonlight effect she was after.

I then asked her how she was going to deal with her

box office earnings. In those very strictly controlled times the Bank of England was certainly not going to let her take a penny out of the country—especially to America, where everyone knew the streets were paved with gold. She replied:

"I'm a show business creature. I have greasepaint in my veins. A normal vacation like other people take would bore me to death. But acting every night in my own play in a country that's new to me . . . that's a vacation! I enjoy every minute of it. Besides, I brought over the whole cast from the States. I have to pay them and the entire cost of the production. There won't be that much left over at the end of the run. But with what there is I shall buy antique silver which I collect and which I'm allowed to take out of the country."

A sophisticated affair

It was a dinner at Maxim's in Paris, and I was late. When I arrived, everyone else was assembled and having drinks. My hostess, understandably annoyed by my lateness, didn't introduce me to any of her other guests.

We went in to dinner, and I was seated next to a handsome woman, older than I by some fifteen years, but still very attractive. I didn't know her name. There were no place cards and during dinner I tried to find out through conversation who she might be. This was not too difficult. She was a divorcee. Her husband had been one of the leading dressmakers of France. He had married again. She had been his first wife.

We danced and I could tell without being conceited that I had made a strong impression on her. It was a Friday, black-tie night at Maxim's. Casually, oh so casually she asked, "What are you doing Saturday night?" I noticed at once that she avoided saying tomorrow night. This would have sounded like rushing things—which, in fact, she was doing.

Feeling very sure of myself, and finding her most attractive, I replied with a piece of calculated impertinence: "Tomorrow night?" (I wasn't going to let that one slip by.) "Why, I'm dining with you." She smiled, taking my insolence with good grace, and said, "Yes, that's about what I was going to suggest."

And so it began. She lived in an exquisite private town house on the Left Bank of Paris, which she'd furnished with superb taste. She had what women so seldom have: taste in furniture as well as in her clothes. She also had the kind of imagination that permitted her to go to the Flea Market to pick up some second-hand shoes of the 1920s and wear them to great effect for a ball or reception. Her feet, incidentally, were exquisite.

I was living at the time quite modestly on the Right Bank. So when we met, which was about every day in the afternoon, it was always at her more comfortable, more luxurious and more convenient home.

Since her divorce she had taken up painting, at which she was remarkably good. Like everything else she did, she injected quality and sophistication into her work.

A short time after our affair had started, she asked me to pose for her. Although her home was spacious, she painted me in her bedroom, and then we made love. Sometimes we made love, and then she painted.

The portrait was almost finished when she said one day: "There is something lacking. I think it's a splashy color. yes, it needs a splash of color somewhere. It is too monochromatic." She went to her vast, mirrored clothes closets and slid the doors open one after the other. Suddenly she came across an evening cape of bright red velvet. It was a gorgeous cape, a gorgeous color, a gorgeous material.

"That's it," she said, pulling it off the hanger, and

throwing it over one of my shoulders. And that is how the painting was finished. It was stunning. There was only one thing wrong with it. I was over thirty years of age, but she made me look like a boy in my early teens, as I might have been at age fifteen, shivering in the cold and selling matches on a street corner. It was a moving portrait.

We were both very satisfied. But she was also a good business woman. "I know exactly who will buy this," she said, and named a French baron well known in Paris society for his impeccable taste and fortune. "But he must not know it is you or he won't buy it. He must think it is some waif I painted on the streets of Naples."

The baron bought the painting.

Although her house was large and the servants' quarters were far from the studio-bedroom, she felt after a while that it would be more discreet if we no longer met there in the afternoons. One day she announced to me that she had made arrangements with a friend of hers, who would be willing to let us use his apartment whenever he was out.

The first time we met there, I felt most uncomfortable. Here I was in the apartment of a man I did not know and who did now know me, using his room, his bed, his bathroom, his soap and towels. On cold afternoons, I even slipped on his dressing gown.

His sheets were made of black silk! And adding to my discomfort was the fact that his valet was always there to answer the doorbell and let us in.

After a while I refused to go there anymore. But my liberated friend had more surprises up her sleeve. We were invited one night, she and I, to a large dressy affair at the house of the Vicomtesse de Noailles. When I came by to pick her up in a taxi, she told me to pay the cab and send it away—we would drive in her car. As she had a low-slung two-seater sports car and was dressed to kill in a ball gown and a tiara on her head this seemed most impractical to me. But she insisted, and we took her car. Soon it became apparent that we weren't heading for the de Noailles house on the Place des Etats Unis.

"Where are we going?" I wanted to know.

"Hush," was all the answer I got. And she drove on until she parked in front of a house where I had never been before. The minute we had crossed the threshold though I got the message. We were in a "discreet" hotel where rooms could be rented by the hour.

The discomfort of having to undress and dress again in such circumstances, when one is wearing a starched shirt, white tie, carnation, and on the distaff side a tiara, pearls, ball gown, long gloves, bra and girdle, is indescribable.

"But why?" I wanted to know when it was all over.

Explanation soon followed.

"I love," she said, and saying so put her hand on my stomach, "this platitude." Her English was not of the best. "And when you came into my sitting room tonight in your tails, I could see the platitude so well. That is why."

We arrived at the Noailles ball hours late, our clothes the worse for what they had suffered, and probably dishevelled and with suspicious rings under our eyes.

But the story doesn't end there. Years later, when everything was quite finished between us, I was in Philadelphia and got a phone call from Mrs. Emlin Etting.

"I'm giving a cocktail party for a visiting fireman from Paris. Won't you come?" And the name she mentioned was that of the man in whose house I had frequently made love in the afternoon. Naturally I went. I wanted to meet him and see if he knew who I was. He didn't. I was one up on him, for I knew that at home in Paris he slept in black satin sheets.

The Begum in Assuan

One evening at Princess Anja Chervachidze's house in Roquebrune, South of France, I found myself sitting next to the Begum Aga Khan, widow of the man who, for years, had been given his weight in gold or precious stone by his religious followers, the Ismaelis. This Begum—for there are several, the old Aga having had four wives—is a beautiful woman who gets ever handsomer as she grows older. I doubt if she could have been so stunning when, as Yvette Labrousse, she was voted Miss France in 1930.

I seized the opportunity of being her table neighbor to ask her a question that had been on my mind for some time.

"I have only been in Egypt once" I said, "and not as far as Assuan. But I have always felt, perhaps unjustly, that it must be deadly dull once one has taken in the usual tourist sights. I know you go there every winter and stay for some time. What do you do all day in Assuan?"

I knew that she had inherited her late husband's villa there, and that he himself was buried nearby. But this in itself didn't seem reason enough for a prolonged sojourn.

"How glad I am you asked me that" she replied. "No one ever asked me before and I am bursting to talk about it. I confess that it is rather boring. Primarily I go to visit my husband's grave. But then I stay on, spending part of every winter. As nothing grows in Assuan, this means a lot of careful preparation. I make lists months ahead at home in Cannes. So many tins of green peas, and so many of something else. I check and double check these lists with my housekeeper, to make sure that nothing has been forgotten. But it never fails: after a few days in Assuan my maid or someone else shows up with a long face and says, 'Really, Princess, we are rather short of rhubarb this year. But there is much too much cranberry juice.'"

"And I think to myself, why couldn't they have told me that back home at my villa Yakamour in Cannes?

"Then there is always at least one occasion when all the lights go out and not one of my staff knows how to repair them. It is my cue to ring up the engineers of the Assuan Dam nearby. Because everyone in Egypt is always most considerate to me, they dispatch one of their officers. He is usually at least a colonel and repairs the damage. After that I have to give a luncheon party for him, on which I had not planned.

But finally the last straw is this: my husband knew Egypt well and had the foresight, when he built our villa, to put in many fireplaces because Egyptian winter nights are cold. It is very pleasant for me to sit by one of these fires after dinner, and read. But when the first wood has died down and I would like to read another chapter, I look at the dying embers and I look at the fresh logs, each one of which has been flown in at great cost from Europe, because there is, of course, no wood of any sort in Assuan, and I say to myself 'To hell with putting another log on the fire' and I close my book and go to bed. I hope this gives you a picture of my life in Assuan."

Somehow this conversation with the usually cool and rather distant Begum made me feel much better and her much more human. It became apparent that the Beautiful People don't always have it all their own way. After that my far simpler life style seemed much easier to bear.

Citizen Kane

I was sitting in Maxim's in Paris, having supper. At another table not far from me I could see Orson Welles and Romy Schneider doing the same. When they had finished their dessert, Romy, like so many of her sex, got up and repaired to the ladies' room to freshen her make-up. Orson was left at his table alone. I took this opportunity to get up and walk over to him, where I introduced myself.

"Mr. Welles," I said, "my name is Franz Hohenlohe and I was a friend of Mr. William Randolph Hearst, which makes me want to ask you a question. I knew both Hearst and Marion Davies well. And they always had the admirable habit of disregarding the disparaging things that people occasionally wrote about them. For instance, Aldous Huxley's "After many a summer dies the swan." But your film *Citizen Kane* offended them deeply. Why were you so bitter in your attacks?

Orson did not hesitate in his answer. "You know," he said, "I never met Mr. Hearst. Not before, and not after *Citizen Kane*. And if it were to be done all over again, I would not shoot that picture. My enmity was inherited from my father, who, for what reasons I never knew, had a terrible, imbedded hatred for Hearst. I simply inherited this antipathy, and now that years have gone by, I am very sorry."

My friend the murderer

My friend, the assassin, was Russian. Actually, it was not so much the assassin who was my friend as his son, Vladimir de Lazovert, a classmate at school and now married to a descendant of Madame Récamier, the lady who gave her name to a sofa.

Dr. Stanislas de Lazovert, the father, was the one who did Rasputin in by slipping a dose of poison into the cakes. He was not alone in doing this. Prince Felix Youssoupoff and the Grand Duke Dimitri were his accomplices. As I knew all three of them, perhaps this vignette should be a plural "my friends the assassins". Grand Duke Dimitri, a handsome man, later became, years after the assassination, the beau of Coco Chanel. He was also a frequent visitor to our home in Paris. As an incumbent historian, I got his assassination story between bouts with my algebra lessons.

Prince Felix Youssoupoff, equally famous for his good looks, in whose palace in Saint Petersburg all this took place, told me the same story of their dark deed at various times during his long life, the last occasion being on the beach of Tangiers.

But back to Stanislas de Lazovert. One of the last times I crossed the Atlantic other than by plane, I was aboard a liner between Cherbourg and New York. Having always hated luxury vessels with their endless

rubbers of bridge, turns around the deck, winds that
blow you all to pieces, and dressing three times a day
for no reason at all, I decided to sit this one out, or
rather lie this one in. From the first day to the last I did
not leave my cabin or my bed. Traveling in style in a
large stateroom, with a private bath, large portholes to
let in fresh air, and bon voyage fruit and flower baskets
aplenty, I had reduced the tedium of crossing to a
minimum. I read and slept and wrote and cut my
toenails. Even so, after three days I had run out of
occupations and of toenails to cut. So I started reading
the passenger list. Like one of Nancy Mitford's
characters, I prefer reading the labels on medicine
bottles to not reading at all. In this fashion I came
across Dr. de Lazovert's name, and picking up the phone
by my bedside I rang him up.

I remembered him from my school days when he
would visit his son at the Collège de Normadie. I knew
what a restless man he was, and how, like me, he must
be suffering from this interminable ocean crossing.
When his voice came on, I could tell at once that he
was seething with impatience to have done with the
tedious journey. Within minutes he was at my cabin
door.

"What on earth are you doing in bed" he quite
naturally wanted to know, the hour being three p.m. I
explained my reasons.

"And you" I said, "what takes you to New York?"

I associated him more with Paris, with Switzerlad,
and with the oilfields of Baku where he was involved

with the Anglo-Iranian Petroleum Company. After feeding the poisoned cakes to Rasputin he had turned to petroleum prospecting and had done very well. Unlike most Russian refugees of the 1917 revolution he had adapted admirably to a new life and was, in fact, a very wealthy man.

"I am on my way to the States to try and see President Truman."

"Oh? What for? Tell me all about it."

"No" he said, "you are too silly and ignorant. You wouldn't understand. It is quite involved." And saying this he got up, and pacing the cabin like a caged tiger, proceeded to tell me everything at great length. His words had not been meant to be offensive. To him I was still the ten-year-old schoolboy he had once known. There was a great deal of unexpressed affection between us, and I understood his restless, high-strung nature. When he had finished, he asked "You wouldn't happen to know anyone in the Truman administration, would you?"

"No. But I do know a very wide-awake banker, Donald Malcolm, who is with the Pew Petroleum people in Philadelphia. I feel he could be instrumental in furthering your interests. Do you want me to introduce you?"

"No, no, I don't," he hastened to say, giving me all the reasons why he felt this Donald Malcolm must be an ignoramous whom it would be a waste of time for him to meet.

So that was that. A day later we landed. I drove

home to 19 East 73rd Street—grandmother Mil's house, which later became the Indonesian Embassy. A few days after our arrival, Lazovert came by to have tea with her. They were old cronies from their school visiting days. While he was there Donald Malcolm was also announced. So the two men met after all, in spite of themselves. Malcolm, whom I had previously told of my meeting with de Lazovert aboard ship, had expressed equally unflattering opinions regarding "Crazy Russians with cockeyed projects!" But when they met it was love at first sight. In fact, they left Mil's house totally engrossed in conversation and in each other. Following this chance encounter they worked together on Lazovert's complex oil deal for several years. With the passing of time, it changed completely from its original concept; but in the end they made a go of it. One day, I was pleasantly surprised to find a four figure check in the mail, as a finder's fee for having introduced them, which in fact I hadn't. How good it is to know certain assassins!

On another of Stanislas de Lazovert's frequent trips to New York, we had a luncheon date at his hotel on East 56th Street. When I got to his apartment he was standing by the living room window looking over Park Avenue. It was past one o'clock, and he was a very punctual man. I wondered why we were not on our way downstairs for lunch?

"What are you waiting for?" I asked.

"The pigeon" was his startling reply.

"The pigeon? What pigeon?"

"The white one. He's late. Most annoying. I feed him on this window sill at twelve thirty every day. I wonder what's keeping him?"

So there was this millionaire businessman who made corporation presidents tremble, this notorious assassin, waiting for a tardy pigeon, showing that under his gruff exterior even an assassin can have a heart of gold.

David Milton

One summer we were all "home on the farm": Steph, Brad Schofield, who was hoping to marry her and whose farm it was, his son and two daughters, his brother, Commander Albert Schofield, and I. This beautiful farm, Anderson Place, dated from 1713. It lies on the Main Line, less than an hour's drive from Philadelphia. Many visitors were in the habit of dropping in on us, especially on weekends. One Sunday it was the turn of David Milton, a millionaire businessman and former husband of a Rockefeller heiress. He'd just flown in from the West Coast and was on his way to New York.

I'd never met Milton before. He was a dynamic man, tall and handsome, with snow white hair. His business interests branched out from aviation to an infinite variety of other activities. One might say that, together with ITT, he was the father of multinationals.

Milton stayed the afternoon with us, and in the evening, when he was ready to start the last lap of his transcontinental journey, it was obvious that he was extremely tired. He asked Steph and Brad Schofield if he could "borrow" me so that I might drive him to New York, as he was afraid of falling asleep at the wheel. This was readily agreed upon, though I was hardly consulted. In fact, I wasn't even given time to change from the blue jeans, tee shirt and sneakers I had worn all day and which smelled strongly of farm manure. Off we went, Mr. Milton and I, in a car he had rented that morning at the airport.

He sat beside me with his eyes closed, his head resting on the back of the seat. But he wasn't sleeping, far from it.

"Start talking" he said quite suddenly.

"What about Mr. Milton?"

"Call me Dave. Oh, anything, Everything that is important to you in life. What, for instance, are your business ambitions?"

As nobody had ever asked me this before, and as I was bursting at the seams with unrequited aspirations, I was delighted. It all came pouring out of me like water from a dam that's burst open. Once in a while I would throw in a question, just to see if he had not fallen asleep. But he hadn't. And occasionally he would interrupt me with a "brilliant" or "atta boy," or he'd say, "We'd better do it slightly differently. That'll save taxes."

By the time we reached New York, fairly late at night, I was sitting on a bright pink cloud. This astute and successful man, a member by marriage of the fabled Rockefellers, had listened for several hours on end to all my pent-up ambitions, ideas, hopes and schemes, and he seemed inclined, judging from the first-person-plural he had used, to implement some of them. It was too good to be true!

"Where do you want to be driven to, Dave?"

We were crossing the Lincoln Tunnel. I visualized

an elegant town house on Fifth Avenue or in the Sixties. But the address he gave me was that of a second rate commercial hotel on lower Park Avenue. I swallowed my surprise and said nothing. Didn't he have a home of his own in New York? And if he lived in a permanent hotel apartment, why on lower Park Avenue

As if he read my thoughts Dave said "This hotel is within walking distance of my office. It's convenient and practical."

When we got there I thought I'd deposit him and then drive home to my own apartment at 30 East 72nd Street. But Dave saw this differently.

"No, you stay right here with me. That way you'll be ready to go to the office with me in the morning."

"But my clothes!" I objected. "I'm wearing dirty jeans and a tee shirt. I can't go to your office like that."

"Yes you can. You can pick up city clothes from your apartment later in the day."

I made another feeble try. "What about getting cleaned up? I don't even have a toothbrush."

"I have dozens of them in their original wrappers. I'll give you one, and soap and a razor." And that was the end of that.

As he spoke he opened the door to his suite. All was dark inside, but the sound of several snores, emanating from various throats and bedrooms, told me we were not alone.

"Who's that?" I asked.

"Oh, probably some of the fellows from the corporation. Maybe Bert from the Nicaragua office or

Dick whom I sent on a mission to Iran last week, or possibly Paul."

All the beds and couches seemed to be occupied except in the master bedroom where I was made to sleep in a small bed alongside of his. Dave threw his clothes in a heap on the floor and within minutes he too was snoring. It took me a while longer to fall asleep in these strange surroundings, and minus the good long shower I had been looking forward to.

The next morning, bright and early, Dave was up. All the other occupants were already gone. Only their unmade beds witnessed the fact that they had really been there. The apartment, now that I had a chance to see it in daylight, was as impersonal as a skating rink. Not a single photograph in a frame, not a flower in any vase, not the slightest memento of anyone or anything.

I put on the same old jeans as the day before, strongly redolent of the barnyard, and followed Dave. Picking up all his clothes of the previous night and throwing them over his arm, he left the apartment with me in tow. On the way to the office we stopped at a dry cleaner's where he exchanged everything he was carrying for a mountain of clean suits, slacks, shirts and socks. Then we continued on to a coffee shop. We were the first customers there. It must have been an all-night place. Breakfast took less time to eat than to order. Soon we were at his office, all three floors of it, on Park Avenue near Grand Central Station. None of his secretaries or any other staff members had yet arrived. I suspect the night watchman had only just left.

Little by little the place started to fill up and I was introduced to everyone. To be truthful, everyone was introduced to me and I felt terribly embarrassed. There was going to be a board meeting within the hour and Dave wanted me to sit in on it, tee shirt and all. Not only that, he encouraged me to voice my opinion if things under discussion did not meet with my approval. From the way he presented me to the board members, as they arrived one by one, it was obvious I had been crowned boy wonder of the day, and they all knew it. But it was also obvious there had been other boy wonders before me. In fact, I met one of them later on. He'd been demoted. I felt I saw his crown still lying in the dust.

My advice was sought and listened to with respect, all that day. If any meals were brought in to us and eaten, I can't say that I remember. Only late at night was I allowed to go home and fetch a change of clothing. But there was no question of my sleeping in my own comfortable 72nd Street bed. Again I was made to spend the night in the master's apartment, sharing his frugal meals, his thoughts, his business, and his strange living routine. I don't think he was aware that other people ate in restaurants, went to the movies, dated girls, played golf, or watched TV.

This went on for a week. Everything I said was noted down in shorthand by some stenographer. Several of my pet projects were discussed in depth and put on a working agenda. When the week was over, Dave was called away on business to a distant part of the world, and I was at last able to return to the comparative peace and quiet of Anderson Place and resume my life where I had left it.

Of my business suggestions I never heard another word. They may have been followed up by the David Milton organization. If so, it was without my knowledge.

I've seen Dave again over the years. On one occasion we found ourselves sitting side by side on a plane between London and New York. Before the stewardesses had served the first round of martinis, he wanted me to change planes with him at Kennedy Airport and continue on right away to South America. With all the affection I have for this remarkable, dynamic, eccentric man, I declined. Let him find another seven-day-wonder-boy, I thought. My sparkling crown must still be lying somewhere in a corner of his Park Avenue office. When we reached New York I drove straight home, before he could shanghai me into flying to South America with him.

Rescue from the sky

It was bitter cold on March 8th, 1958 in Brandywine, Pennsylvania, and I was traveling from New York City to Ohio for a lecture engagement. The weather forecast had been bad, and trains and planes not having connections to the small college town in which I was to lecture, the best bet to insure arriving on time had seemed to be a Greyhound bus.

I had boarded my bus in New York, late at night. It must have been close to midnight, and I had promptly fallen asleep, being one of those fortunate people who can sleep anytime, anywhere, lying, sitting, or standing up. After a restful number of hours I woke up, opened one eye and both my ears. Something was wrong. What was it? Oh yes, there was no noise at all and we were standing still. With the one open eye I looked out the window and saw that everything around us was white—approximately halfway up the side of the bus. Outer Siberia could not have been whiter. Everyone else was still asleep, except for the driver who sat at the wheel in total resignation. I walked up to him and asked, "What's up?"

"We're snowed in."

"What are you going to do about it?"

"Your guess is as good as mine. Wait for help."

That didn't sound promising. While talking I had

noticed the rooftop of a farmhouse peeking out of the snow in a field a few hundred yards from the turnpike we were on.

"Do you think the people in that house over there could help us?" I said, more to myself than to him.

"Doin' what?" he replied. "Nobody can dig us out of this kinda snow. It's just as bad ahead as it is here."

"They might give us some food or at least hot water to make coffee."

"You wanna try, you go ahead" he answered.

By this time our voices had awakened several other passengers. A small team of men came forward, and with newspapers wrapped around our feet, to try and keep them from getting sopping wet, we ventured forth. The snow reached well over our hips, and getting to the farmhouse took us about fifteen minutes. When we reached it we found, to our great disappointment, that is was empty and boarded up. However, I thought I could make out the faint whining of a dog somewhere inside. Some unmentionable swine had locked up that dog inside the house before leaving, with the intention of letting him starve to death. When I heard that noise I was determined to get inside and rescue the helpless animal. I tried all around the house and finally got in through one of the back windows, badly boarded up and easy to break through. Inside the totally empty house I was greeted by a friendly tail wagging young police dog. The owners of the farm could not have left very long before, and he was, thank God, still in good physical shape. After he had licked my face quite copiously and I had spoken words of encouragement to him, I went around looking for something that would give me a clue to the name of his owners. I was in luck. There, by the door, was some mail, obviously pushed through the slot after their departure. I took one of the advertising circulars and slipped it into my pocket. Then I pushed the dog through the window and followed him out. The two of us made our way back to the stranded bus where some travelers who had some food were sharing it with those who did not have any. We ate an improvised breakfast of Nabisco, peanuts, and Seven Up. My dog got some of this bounty, too, and looked grateful.

Our wait lasted all day. In late afternoon a helicopter flew overhead and was our first sign of a prospective rescue. But there were, of course, many hundreds of motorists in the same predicament as we, all along the turnpike, hidden from our view by the mountains of snow. The helicopter must have touched down a few miles ahead for we could see and hear its frequent trips to and fro. The first to be rescued were all those in bad health, requiring quick evacuation. Several people had suffered heart attacks. A few of them died. There were also some pregnant women. They were all evacuated first. Then came the elderly, not yet called senior citizens, followed by women and children. And finally the able-bodied men.

By the time it was my turn, night had fallen. But the helicopter crew decided I looked too healthy to be rescued. Besides, they refused to take the dog, and I was not going to fly off without him. I was left standing in the snow with my new four-legged companion, until a snowplow came and gave us a lift. I was probably the last man to be evacuated. The ignominy of being rescued by a snowplow! But when I tell the story now, I always call it my helicopter rescue, which sounds much better.

Everyone had been taken to a Howard Johnson restaurant, which was overflowing so much that we could not all lie down, or even sit down at the same time, and we took turns sleeping on the floor or standing. During one of my standing periods I made arrangements by phone to turn my dog companion over to the SPCA, with the proviso that they find a good home for him. We had by then become very fond of each other and our parting was sad. He kept looking back at me.

My last act in this drama was turn in the names of the brutal former owners of the dog and denounce them for their cruelty. After that I made my exit, on another bus and on roads partly cleared of snow, and feeling much better.

Paul Getty

I met Jean Paul Getty on very few occasions, but these sufficed as far as I was concerned. The first time I was scheduled to meet him, an American friend, Lady Clifford, wife of Sir Bede Clifford, onetime Governor of the Bahamas and Mauritius, rang up from her country house in Sussex. I was living in London, working for a Swiss Bank in the City.

"Come out for lunch on Sunday," she said. "The weather is so lovely it would be a shame if you stayed in town."

The luncheon was small. Only one other guest had been invited, a lady who had come down from London as had I. During our meal Alice informed us, "I'm taking you two over to Paul Getty's this afternoon. I thought you might be interested to see what the old boy has done to Sutton Place since he bought it. He wants us to have tea with him."

The Cliffords' country house, Queen Ann Farm, lay within easy driving distance from Mr. Getty's historic home, Sutton Place, where King Henry VIII had courted Ann Boleyn before making her his second wife and later chopping off her head. It so happened that all three of us had known the previous owner, the Duke of Sutherland, and were consequently acquainted with the lovely Tudor house and its sumptuous interior.

When we arrived at Sutton Place later in the afternoon, the butler opened the door and, addressing Alice Clifford, said, "Your Ladyship, Mr. Getty will not be coming downstairs."

I thought it very odd that he did not say, "Mr. Getty sends his regrets but won't be coming downstairs," or, "Mr. Getty is indisposed and apologizes for not being able to come downstairs."

Any number of variations crossed my mind. But certainly, had I been Mr. Getty, I would have seen fit to instruct my butler to say more than the few words of bare civility which had been spoken—especially since Alice was an old friend, a neighbor, and a lady. Fortunately, like many other Americans, Lady Clifford was up to any situation. Stepping undaunted past him she threw over her shoulder, "Never mind, Hormsby, I shall show my guests around myself."

The Butler retired and we were given the grand tour most efficiently, by Alice herself. She pointed out Getty's new acquisitions and told us many interesting historical details in such a way that old man Getty's absence was not felt at all. In the course of our visit we came face to face with a large painting so very like one that I owned myself that I was thunderstruck. Although the one hanging at Sutton Place was quite a bit bigger than mine, everything about it reminded me of the canvas at home in my London flat. A dark country scene with a gloomy sky, as though a thunderstorm was looming. On a pond some ducks (in my picture they are swans) were being barked at by a pack of hounds on the embankment. After the tour we were not offered tea and soon departed, each one of us too well brought up to say what we thought of Mr. Getty's hospitality.

Back in London, I lost no time in calling up an art dealer expert to come and have a look at my painting and authenticate it. The expert I chose was a friend, Mr. Paul Larsen of Duke Street. My painting and Mr. Getty's were undoubtedly seventeenth or eighteenth century. That much I could tell myself. And both were unquestionably by the same artist. It remained to be seen if Mr. Getty's painting and mine were done by a "name" painter. Seeing how fine a collection of pictures hung at Sutton Place, this seemed more than likely.

Paul Larsen took one look at my painting and said, without a moment's hesitation "You have an Oudry. Jen-Baptiste Oudry, 1686-1755. Your picture is probably worth £10,000 at today's prices."

That was all I wanted to know. I was elated and took Paul Larsen to lunch. I then had a small plaque affixed to the picture's frame, with the name and date of the artist. It hangs today in my home in California.

Not long after this, the Duchess of Bedford rang me up. "We're giving a ball at Woburn Abbey. Want to come?"

As French-born Nicole Bedford is one of the most fun people I know, brim full of energy and a fabulous organizer, I accepted at once. "Come early" she said, "I want you to have dinner with us before the ball."

The dinner before the Bedford's ball boasted the

presence of two of the world's richest men, Nubar Gulbenkian and Paul Getty. Gulbenkian did not interest me at all. I had always considered him a ridiculous fop and publicity hound who would do anything to attract attention and get his picture into the papers. Who else would go riding to hounds with a spray of orchids in his buttonhole? Besides, in spite of always being called "Mr. Five Per Cent" by the press, he had not earned a penny of his money. It was all accumulated by his father. Paul Getty, however, interested me because of our two Oudry paintings. I went up to him as we were having cocktails and introduced myself.

"I owe you a debt of gratitude, Mr. Getty" I said. "The other day when Lady Clifford was showing me around your house (I did not add "and you behaved like a churlish lout by not coming downstairs"), I saw an Oudry you own, and this enabled me to identify one I have myself, although I did not realize it."

Anyone with a modicum of education would, at that point, have made a simple noncommittal remark such as "Oh, I'm so glad" or "Isn't that nice." Mr. Getty did no such thing. He looked at me with his cold fish eyes staring out of that surgically lifted face of his, as though I were an unsavory type of vermin. Then he turned on his heels and walked away.

I'm sorry to have to relate that this was still not the end of my run-ins with Mr. Getty. There was one more. Again I was rung up by a woman friend of mine. This time it was Susan Eddy. Mrs. Eddy was an old lady who had been a friend of my family's and knew me as a child. She was a widow and rather keen on organizing charity affairs.

"Do me a favor, dear child" she began, "I am an old woman and men of my age bore me to extinction. So won't you please be my escort for the Sailors' Benefit Ball of which I am chairman?"

And she would have died rather than use the ridiculous newfangled "chairperson".

"It will be no fun for you at all, I know. But you will be doing this old gal a tremendous favor."

"Suzy" I said, "You are more fun than a brace of nincompoop debs. Besides, I love you. Of course I'll come."

Mrs. Eddy had been chairman of this ball for over a quarter of a century and ran it most efficiently. Her party that night consisted of about ten people. We all met at her house for cocktails and then proceeded to the Savoy Hotel where the ball was being held. As chairman, Mrs. Eddy wanted us to be there before the doors leading to the ballroom were opened. Consequently, we were the first arrivals and stood there chatting and waiting. Besides us, a solitary male in evening clothes was also standing there in a lonely corner. Oddly, he had his back turned to the lobby and was staring into the wall like a naughty pupil at school who was being punished. All he needed to complete this illusion was a dunce's cap on his head. No one in our party paid the slightest attention to him, and no one commented on the oddity of his bearing. But to my eagle eyes, it seemed as if I recognized the back of J.

Paul Getty's head. Pretty soon a young woman in evening clothes came up to this odd figure, and they had a whispered conversation. She then walked over to Mrs. Eddy and introduced herself.

"I am Mr. Paul Getty's secretary," she said. Mr. Getty wants me to ask you to make quite sure that he will not be molested by autograph seekers. He also does not wish to be photographed. And would you please see to it that he has a table near the entrance so that he can leave at any time without crossing the ballroom."

It was quite obvious that this poor young thing, who had the misfortune of being Getty's secretary, was delivering this extraordinary recitation with great misgivings, as she was blushing and stammering all the time she was doing so. Susan Eddy meanwhile had been growing taller and taller by the second. She was a regal figure of a woman by nature, but now had grown eight feet tall.

Her face remained perfectly composed. When the hapless secretary finished delivering her message, Susan said to her very calmly, "My sweet young woman, I have run this charity for a quarter of a century, and during this time I have had many people of note attending it. The Duchess of Kent has been to it several times. The Queen has graciously accepted to be among us, and Mr. Noel Coward has charmed us as a witty M.C. Should anyone have asked for their signature I'm sure they would have willingly given them. As for photographers, I cannot control the press and certainly would not wish to were I able. So please go over and tell your employer," and with that she pointed the accusing finger of the Archangel Gabriel in Getty's direction without glancing at him, "that not only will I be glad to see that he gets the table nearest the entrance, but I can arrange for him to leave by that entrance without attending my ball at all."

These words were delivered in a clear voice that would have filled Carnegie Hall. It was quite obvious to us, who were the delighted spectators of this scene, that Susan Eddy, although she'd seemed oblivious of the ridiculous figure standing in his corner, had known all along who he was. I felt terribly sorry for the unfortunate young secretary who was, after all, only doing her duty. But then that comes from working for men like Paul Getty.

And did he leave after that? No, he didn't.

The murder of Aliette

I was in Vienna. It was winter. There was snow on the ground and it was unpleasantly cold. Not the cold of the great outdoors, but the nagging, slushy cold of a city. And I, for what reason I can no longer remember, was staying at the Palais Schönburg. Probably I had promised Lily Schönburg, to whom I was distantly related—her mother and Aglae Hohenlohe being sisters—that I would stay at their dreary, drafty, decaying Schönburg palace as a paying guest on my next visit to Vienna.

Just as I arrived from Paris and was stepping out of my taxi, Princess Lily and her younger sister were departing from the Semmering, Vienna's nearest skiing resort, to spend New Year's Eve with Thornton Wilder. They invited me to join them, and I would have given anything to meet Thornton Wilder, whose books I loved. But I was tired, cold, hungry, and in need of a bath. I declined. So there I was, all alone on New Year's Eve, in that forbidding mausoleum, with only a Greek Orthodox Pope who seemed to have been hired to do all the housework. He lit my fire in a wood burning porcelain stove once a day, in the morning, and after that I was alone.

It was too much. Feeling desperately sorry for myself I left on the third day and took off for the civilized comforts of the Hotel Sacher. Once there, I began ringing up all my friends and relatives and gradually thawed into what I consider a normal way of life. One of those I called was Princess Aliette de Rohan. I invited her to dinner. She was then working in an office, as her family, the noble and prestigious Rohans, had lost everything with the arrival of the Russian troops at the end of the war. I also invited a young Hungarian, quite a few years younger than Aliette, and of an excellent gentry family. Our dinner was a great success. My two guests got along well and the following morning I spoke with her over the phone.

"You know Aliette," I said, "I'll give you Gyula's address and telephone number, because a single woman like you, tied down to an office job during the day, often needs a last minute escort for a dinner engagement or as a fourth at bridge. As he is very pleasant and presentable, I think you'd do well to have him in your files in case you need him."

But she surprised me by saying, "I'm sorry Franzi, but I could never go out with him here in Vienna. He has no title."

I could hardly believe my ears, because, although Vienna is admittedly snobbish, it is not usually that snobbish.

A few years went by. Aliette came to France to live and work. Again I invited her, this time to my apartment in Paris and also to the Ritz for lunch. I had by then founded my own men's clothing manufacturing business, and was always in need of good sales representatives to send on the road. I had sales reps covering France, England, Switzerland, Austria, Italy and the Benelux countries. Some were good. Many were not. One who was excellent as far as aggressiveness and sales were concerned was Michel de Genouillac. He was also stubborn as hell and hard to control. He came from a good family but was really a gangster at heart—so much so that when I found out he was selling counterfeit garments from my collections, behind my back and under a different label, I fired him.

Unknown to me, Aliette and Michel had met at some cocktail party. And, strange to relate, for a woman as fiercely class conscious as she, they had started a romance. He was then 25, Aliette over 40. In time what had to happen happened. Faced by his incessant rudeness and bad manners, Aliette put an end to their affair. But they remained on speaking terms and occasionally still saw each other.

One evening, returning to her apartment after work in the car of another secretary from her office, Aliette mentioned casually that Michel was coming to dine with her. In fact, she asked her friend to drop her off at a liquor store as she was out of Scotch, which he liked to drink. Michel showed up for dinner and while sipping his highball they began to quarrel over his habit of putting his feet on the table. Aliette was incensed, as she always was when he did this.

"If you can't respect the lady in me, then at least respect the woman," she said, pulling his feet from the table.

"If you're going to get on your high horse," he replied, "I'll leave now and not have dinner with you."

"Suit yourself," she countered.

Before he left he entered the bathroom and performed what people go to bathrooms for, without closing the door behind him. This was done deliberately, and quite typical of him. Aliette, infuriated by the exhibition, took hold of the first object that she could lay her hands on. It happened to be a small aerosol mace he himself had once given her in case she was ever attacked in the street. She now squirted this in his face. He, in turn, took hold of the nearest object to hand, the bottle of whisky she had just bought, and hit her over the head with it until she dropped dead at his feet. Then, quite slowly and deliberately, he went about collecting several valuable objects, opening cupboards and drawers, to make the scene look like a burglary. He put everything in a suitcase and left.

Although the apartment building was large and there were many tenants in it, nobody saw Michel leave. He drove to a railway station and deposited the stolen belongings in a locker. After that he bought a large jerrycan at a service station. Driving to a second service station, he had the can filled with gasoline and returned, unperturbed, to Aliette's apartment to which he still had the key. He proceeded to pour gasoline over her body and the rest of the room and set fire to it. Again, incredibly, nobody saw him as he emerged. The entire floor went up in flames, threatening the whole building.

As he had some examinations to pass the following morning, he drove back to the home of his parents where he was still living, and began calmly cramming for the next day. But not without having first washed the clothes he was wearing which had been splattered by Aliette's blood. Next day he sat for his examinations and passed them successfully.

If it had not been for the friend who drove Aliette home on the afternoon of the murder, and to whom she had mentioned that Michel was coming for dinner, he would probably never have been suspected and would still be free today. As it is he is now spending time in a French jail—but will most certainly be released soon for "good behavior."

Murray Korda

My old friend, Los Angeles society band leader Murray Korda, is a great jokester. There was an occasion when he succeeded in embarrassing me under the table, so to speak. It happened at a big dinner and dance in Palm Springs. For what reason I'm sure I don't know I had been seated in the place of honor at the head table, which stood on a raised platform overlooking the dance floor and all the other tables in the large ballroom. This head table was also, quite naturally, facing the stage where Murray and his band were playing for us that evening.

When we had finished dessert and after-dinner coffee was being served to us, the room was plunged into darkness and the floor show began. I considered this an auspicious moment to get up unnoticed and repair to the men's room. I assumed that no one would notice my absence. When I returned to my seat, all the lights had been turned on again, the first part of the evening's entertainment was finished, and Murray, up on his stage, was making an announcement. I caught him saying my name and stopped in my tracks to listen.

"Franzi" I heard him say, looking straight at me, "here I am dedicating beautiful music to you. And where are you during that time? In the loo."

I turned scarlet—especially as I think I was still

finishing zipping up my fly. All eyes turned toward me, and everyone doubled up with laughter. The evening was a great success.

Another evening, another dance, this one the always lovely Vienna Opera Ball at the Beverly Wilshire Hotel. My date and I are waltzing by the stage where Murray is leading his musicians. But his back is not turned to the ballroom, and he sees me, gives me a huge wink, steps off the stage, comes up to me and gives me two resounding smackers, one on each cheek. Another couple, also dancing by, seeing all this, raises their eyebrows to the ceiling and lets out, "Well!"

This doesn't faze Murray at all. He grins from ear to ear and counters with, "It's all right. My wife knows all about it."

Pitz

I have a friend whose name is Hermann Broch de Rothermann. He was in the same school as I, though slightly before, being older. This friend is the son of the celebrated Austrian author-philosopher Hermann Broch. The Rothermann part comes from his mother's side of the family. But all his friends call him Pitz, which is a good deal simpler.

The women in Pitz's life would fill several telephone directories. They have included tall ones and short ones, plump ones and slim ones, rich ones and poor ones. Some were auburn, some brunette, blonde, and red-headed. Even the German mistress of the King of Albania was among them.

And yet his methods of conquest are hardly subtle. He simply goes straight for the target. There we were sitting one night, he and I and a lot of other people, around a dinner table in some ballroom. Sitting between us was an amiable fat blob. I had not paid the slightest attention to her, although her skin, I must admit, as is so often the case with fat people, was smooth and quite beautiful. It wasn't long before Pitz leaned over to me, as though she were not present, and said "Have you ever seen anything to compare with that lovely skin?" And saying this his eyes strayed unmistakably into her cleavage. The fat one giggled and became slightly pink in her face, but not much. That was enough for Don Juan Pitz.

"May I?" he asked, and plunged his hand, before she had time to say anything, into the full roundness of her corsage. "I have seldom come across such perfection," he continued, before she could catch her breath—during which interlude his right hand was foraging beneath her textile. But the lady was still not protesting at all.

"Like satin and velvet" Pitz continued. Finally the satin and velvet-skinned one opened her mouth in mild protest.

"Naughty boy" she said. That was all. But she did nothing to stop his auscultation.

When I saw him the following morning I thought it fitting to give him a piece of my mind.

"Aren't you ashamed?" I asked. "Such a balloon of a girl! And her rear filled the entire chair she sat on!"

"Maybe" he replied. "But did you have a better one at hand?"

That then is my school friend, Pitz von Rothermann. On a quite different occasion we were in Cuba together. It was winter. Out of season. He and I were sitting in a Greyhound bus in Havana, on our way to a resort called Varadero, which we already knew and liked, and which would be quite empty of tourists at this time of year. It was late afternoon and we sat in darkness, waiting for the bus to depart, when at the last minute one more passenger hopped in through the open door. All one could make out in that poor light was that this passenger

*"Pitz" with Yvonne Larsen at the
author's (rented) Chateau de Chatel.*

was female, but whether she was young or old, pretty or ugly, could not be distinguished. She sat down behind us and the bus started moving. So did Pitz's right hand. It was terribly occupied behind him, in the darkness. That hand, I mean. This started a gay dialogue between the unknown quantity and himself, for Pitz—an interpreter at the United Nations at the time—speaks very good Spanish. With the help of his Spanish and his right hand, he seemed to be doing pretty well for himself. I, who have witnessed him a thousand times in similar circumstances, fell asleep. Halfway between Havana and Varadero the lady in the dark alighted from the bus. Pitz, true to his Casanova nature, immediately blotted her from his mind.

The following afternoon we were sitting on the empty beach in front of our hotel, just the two of us, when from a distance we made out a female form — a damned good one I will say — who seemed to be waving in our direction. Although we knew that there was no one behind us, we both looked over our shoulders. No, indeed, the hotel beach was empty. Meanwhile the young lady of the good silhouette came nearer, still waving, straight towards us, or should I say towards Pitz? Now only did we get a good look at her. She was black as coal, and very pretty. Her teeth were white, her legs were slim, her bosom, A-1. At last she was standing before us and let herself down in the sand, but not for long, because Pitz decided that the climate in his room would be healthier for both her and him.

"Goodbye," he said, "See you later," as he walked

off with his conquest of the day before, since obviously that's who she was. Although he had no recollection of it, he had arranged this date with her on the bus the preceding afternoon.

The sun was slowly going down, and finally I, too, left the beach and returned to my room at the hotel. My room and Pitz's were adjacent. The hotel, quite old and very charming, was built of wood at a time when no one had yet heard of acoustic insulation. What went on next door could be heard as clearly as though there were no wall to separate one room from the next. The noises I heard confirmed to me, if I needed it, that their conversation was not intellectual. Far from it. Violent groans and sighs reached my ears quite distinctly. But finally they stopped, and Pitz, clad in a bath towel like a Roman emperor, came into my room.

"Give me thirty bucks" he said.

"Are you out of your cotton picking mind?" I countered. "Why should I give you thirty bucks?"

"Because I haven't any money in my room, and I have to give the poor thing some money for her return fare. She is a chambermaid in a private family, and today was her day off." And saying this he marched toward my wallet which most unfortunately was lying on the table, and extracted thirty dollars from it. I was outraged.

"You have all the fun and I have to pay for it!"

"Miser" he said, and walked out the door. As for the thirty dollars, I doubt he ever paid them back to me. I hope he will when he reads this.

Finis

I have always been very ecologically minded, which in our family is hereditary. My Aunt Milla, in the days when dray horses could still be seen on the streets of big cities, would not hesitate to snatch the whip from the hands of the coachman, if she felt he brutalized his horses, and whip him with it. Pop had a language all his own with which he only addressed his dächshunds. Great Aunt Clotilde chewed steak before giving it to her Pekingese, to make it more digestible for them. Mil put compresses around her poodle's neck when the vet said he had a sore throat. Steph would jump out of any vehicle she was in, even when on the way to the opera all decked out in expensive finery, if she saw a dog she judged to be lost, and immediately adopt it.

There is not much in nature that I don't like, from sunrise to sundown, from hot sand to cold snow, and I have a soft spot in my heart for all animals, with special emphasis on dogs, horses, deer, does, dolphins, giraffes and elephants. See me kissing an elephant on his trunk, on the next page. As for dolphins, I have already ridden on their backs in Florida, and intend to do so again.

I cannot understand how it is possible that there are still people in the world who have not understood that we depend on animals and animals depend on us

A soft spot for
everything in nature.

for survival of Earth, in the ecological chain. That there should still be some people who hunt animals which are on the endangered species list not only revolts me, but leaves me wondering whether they have quite undestood what our fight is all about.

But more than their total extinction, it is the cruelty to animals which revolts me most. In Spain there is a provincial town where, on a given day each year, the city notables pick the oldest donkey, and on his back they place the fattest man they can find in the city. The poor beast, if his back is not broken right from the start, is then driven through the town, among the rejoicing populace. People pour boiling water over him, stick spears into his side, and pierce his eyes. All this among clamours and loud ribaldry. At the end of this triumphant ride the obese rider gets off the donkey's back—if the wretched animal is still alive—and the crowd applauds him. The donkey is left in some corner to die. In the hope that my feeble voice might be of some help, I have written to King Juan of Spain, the grandson of my old friend Queen Ena, to beseech him to put a stop to this mediaeval practice.

I have also solicited the help of His Royal Highness the Duke of Edinburgh, whose sister was married to the head of our Hohenlohe-Langenburg branch, since at the head of WWF there is a great deal he can do.

If in writing these lines I have helped to stop only a fraction of the evil actions in the world, I shall be happy.

INDEX

The author's immediate family and various household staff, who are featured throughout this book, are not included in these listings:

Lazovert, Vladimir de, 251
Laver, James, 102
Ledebur, Count Frederick, 118
Lehner, George, 201, 206-208
Lobb, 72, 84
Lopokova, Lydia, 118-121
Lubitsch, Ernst, 152
Luce, Clare, 131
Ludwig I, King of Bavaria, 118
Maraini, Fosco, 213-215
Majlath, Countess, 26
Malcom, Donald, 253-254
Maraini, Fosco, 205
Martinez de Hoz, Dulcie, 74
Mecklenburg,
  Prince Henry of, 18
Mercati, Countess, 88
Milton, David, 256-261
Mitford, Nancy, 252
Moore, Grace, 163
Moore, Sir Thomas, 110, 112
Muller, Maitre Mathieu, 190
Muñoz, Madame, 74
Mussolini, 62, 90
National Socialist Party
  (Nazis), 110, 123-124, 168-169,
  173
Negri, Pola, 152-154
Negyessy de Szepessy, Baron
  Kálman, 26
Niven, David
Nizam of Hyderabad, 122
Noailles, Vicomtesse de, 88
Obolensky, Prince Alexander,
  120
Obolensky, Princess Irena,
  120, 122-126

Oporto, Duchess of, 103-105
Overell, Eric, 90
Oxford, Lady Margot, née
  Tennant, Margot (Countess
  of Oxford and Asquith),
  87-90, 92, 100
Paquin, 72
Park, Harold,
  159-161, 183-184
Park, Madeline,
  159-161, 164, 183-185
Pavlova, Anna, 13
Pedroso, Counts de, 40-43
Pépé le Moko, 159
Perier, Count du, de Larsan, 111
Perona, John, 104-105
Perugia, Signor, 72-74
Pignatelli, Princess Conchita,
  150
Pinza, Ezio, 121, 163
Pius XI, Pope, 55-59
Plan-les-Ouates, Geneva, 71
Platz, Count Ludwig, 122
Pogany, Willy, 150
Polunin, Nicolas, 94
Polunin, Professor, 94-95
Rainier du Monaco, 92, 118
Rasputin, 251
Rassponi, Count Lanfranco,
  163
Récamier, Madame, 251
Redeker, Frank, 182
Richter, Dr. Johannes, 26
Rohan, Princess Aliette de,
  273-277
Roosevelt, President Franklin,
  156, 166